A Little
Goes a Long Way

by
James 'Tiny' Little

To

Ivan .
Best wishes

Tiny

ISBN 978-0-9566242-0-8

Printed by Barnwell Print Ltd of Aylsham, Norfolk NR11 6SU

Foreword

The world of Ocean Rowing is full of characters. The first thing you need to know about Tiny is that James 'Tiny' Little is to Ocean Rowing what 'Little' John was to Robin Hood! The first time I met Tiny was in Edinburgh when he was up to watch the Calcutta Cup rugby match with his friend David Blake. The lovely Yvette Jelfs and I lived in Edinburgh at the time and I had heard of his voyage so we agreed to get together for a pre match 'sharpener' or five! This powerfully built, tall Englishman entered our home with a kilt on. As the many 'sharpeners' took effect I remember thinking quietly to myself as a Scotsman 'Thank God! He looks like he's on our side!'.

It was not long before I was graciously invited to his pub (the famous 'Alex' in picturesque Norwich) and as that evening played out and the 'CHB' went down I grew to understand, like the many that know him, this was a very rare and special man, quietly but unconquerably determined, modest and strong, slow to anger and quick to forgive. I also knew that a friendship was formed over the initial kinship of our respective voyages that would last for as long as there was breath in our lungs and waves on the ocean.

Tiny has that effect on people.

Solo Ocean Rowing was not 'invented' until the late 1960's. It was not until John Fairfax rolled up on Hollywood Beach, Florida on the 19th of July 1969 and Tom McClean arrived safe in Blacksod Bay, Ireland only days later, that people even dared to think it was possible. Until quite recently more people had set foot on the moon than had rowed an ocean alone and unaided. In those early days loved ones waved 'goodbye' from the quayside and then hoped, their eyes telling us all what their mouths dare not say.

Today the pictures are digital, enhanceable, cropable and e-mailable! But I would encourage you to look into these old tattered black and white photographs of the early days of Ocean Rowing, then tell me the scenes are not the same. Human beings have not changed much we still blister, burn, bleed and hurt. Families at home still wonder and worry - and so to the Ocean we go. The beautiful place.

This raw, untainted, diarised account is written with Tiny's usual modesty and humour but I would urge you, in places, to stop and read between the lines to better understand what a truly great feat this was. I humbly submit that some of the descriptions are so vivid, accurate and enthralling that it is not like reading an account. It is like you were actually there!

When I first read this book I did so without break from start to finish. It took me, as it will you, on an emotional journey of the highs and lows of this simply remarkable achievement. You will laugh out loud and you may even shed a tear.

You are about to take a seat beside Tiny as he rows across the Atlantic Ocean raising money for the Davenport Trust and on a voyage of discovery.

Prepare yourself to board the Womble ...

Leven Sinclair-Brown.
Solo Atlantic Ocean rower 2005/6.
Captain, La Mondiale, World record Atlantic row 2007/8

John Fairfax. The first solo rower   *Photo courtesy of Ocean Rowing Society*

Sidney Genders Atlantic 1969-70   *Photo courtesy of Ocean Rowing Society*

What follows is the day by day account of an ocean row. It was produced daily, on a laptop inside the tiny cabin of an ocean rowing boat in sometimes extreme conditions. It contains grammatical and spelling errors and it is to a very large extent raw material. To edit the text would in my humble opinion, take away something of the adventure.

The log does differ slightly from the account on my website because the web version was dictated daily to an answer machine at home, it was then typed out by my wife Anita, then e-mailed to Ian Stutely, the webmaster for posting live. The satellite phone link was difficult to hear at times and some errors were included.

Wednesday 19 January 2005
The forecast is not good, the winds tomorrow are not safe for me to leave and I may have to postpone until Monday. I'm deeply unhappy about this, but it has to be done for the safety of the project and myself. I intend to use the time fixing last minute snags and trying to get the computers to talk to the telephone. I have been working on this problem for ages now and it is getting to me a bit. I know that it is the elusive correct stroke of a key, but I really do want to keep my website live from the ocean, and it looks as if it might not happen.

Thursday 20 January 2005
I have just seen the forecast for the weekend and have decided to leave at 10am tomorrow. The boat is now ready, all ballast is in and hatches tight. I will get a few fresh provisions from the supermarket in the morning and GO!

Happy birthday Dave the frock, and Vince Collymore in Barbados!

Friday 21 January 2005

Left berth in San Sebastian de La Gomera at 1000. Rowed slowly out after Alex gave me the last mooring rope. As I rowed out of the marina I was waved off by many new friends including three young children who had delighted in running up and down the berth pontoon for a week shouting "Hola!" at the boat and me. As I turned the corner into the harbour I was met by two yachts to escort me outbound. One, Silver Wind,belonged to Pete Dawson, the other to the Canary sailing school and crewed by their latest class, a bevy of beautiful Irish ladies. crossing the start line on my left I had the ladies singing the Womble song and on my right the Alex crew with horns and party poppers.

I felt really quite emotional on my way out, but an hour later the yachts had gone and the adventure began with a start; a south easterly wind blew up at the same time that my hangover kicked in. If I didn't row hard now, I would be blown straight back into harbour to start over again. I refused to allow that to happen and rowed solidly for seven hours into the wind to clear the ferries and the land. As soon as I felt clear enough I flopped off my seat and lay on deck for half an hour. What a way to begin; so much for the long slow build up. My muscles will be reminding me about this tomorrow.

Saturday 22 January 2005

I put out the sea anchor last night and slept much more soundly than I would have expected. I was woken at 3am by a ship passing close by, and I saw that the wind had shifted, so I immediately took the oars and rowed South. At 5am the wind died away, so I turned in until 8am. When I rose Tenerife and La Gomera had gone! A haze hid what was left of their visibility so I was on my own at sea, in the smallest boat in the marina setting out to cross an ocean. The Womble which had seemed so big outside the pub now felt very small indeed.

Stiffness from the big audition yesterday has been a nuisance, but if I keep stretching and rowing it will soon go.

Hallucinations have started already, I am hearing dogs bark and children shouting, this evening a man behind me called out "Callum", but I didn't reply, well it isn't my name.

Sunday 23 January 2005
The day was spent trying out rowing techniques whilst trying to avoid El Hierro, an island to the south west of me. I have been rowing at right angles to the wind and sea which I find difficult, still, a more productive day than others, the trip meter shows 45 miles to date. North easterlies coming soon?

Monday 24 January 2005
Today was very sunny and hot - 90 fahrenheit. Flat calm all day with a half knot push from the Canary current. I made water, washed my shirt, tidied the cabin and began to make a half tidy vessel. I listened to Albert Cooper, ate beef teriyaki and wore my bow tie for dinner, but I have not yet opened the wine cellar.

Happy birthday Andy Lowe, my ornithological coach.

Tuesday 25 January 2005
Yesterday we made 30 miles in the day which is my target for each day. I rewarded myself with an orange. No oranges for today though, only 20 miles. However it is Burns night, so the wombles and I celebrated in style and had haggis, which I piped in and addressed in the traditional way, with a dram.
Trip reading, 90 miles.

Wednesday 26 January 2005
Calm all morning and rowing well but at about 3pm a north westerly wind came which made conditions difficult. I put out the big boy (sea anchor) and spent the rest of the day being bounced around. In the forenoon I was joined by the most inquisitive school of Dolphins which stayed with me for over an hour. They were about twenty in number and had youngsters with them. They came right up to the boat and brushed the oars and rudder, they jumped and played around and when I stopped rowing they just stayed with me. One lifted its head above the water for some time, just watching me. I took a couple of photos, and starterd rowing again, they followed for a while then went away.

Happy birthday Harriet!

Trip 102 miles

Thursday 27 January 2005
Spent all last night and all morning on the big boy, with no change in the wind direction, but an increase in strength. The Womble has been airborne twice today! Both times within fifteen minutes, I was laid in the cabin listening to the racket (not a punk band) when I felt suddenly weightless. A second later we hit the water with a mighty crash. This was repeated ten minutes later .No damage done, but one freeze dried meal missing presumed lost.

This afternoon I noticed that my right sock was inside-out, now us Sagittarians are not given to superstition but as soon as I turned it the right way out the wind eased! So, my right sock is now my wind sock.

Thank you all for the text messages you sent, they really are very welcome.
Trip 111 miles

Friday 28 January
Started rowing at 6am today, lasted until 0900 when I had to stop for rough sea. I started again at 1200 and made reasonable progress through the afternoon despite fairly high seas. I am learning to surf in a rowing boat., no easy task.

My progress still seems very slow but I'm not worried about that, conditions will change sooner or later.
Trip 131 miles

Saturday 29 January
What a day. By 0830 the rowing was over. I tried four times more in the course of the day but there was no chance of making any progress, so the big para anchor went out and I stayed in the cabin through the night being bounced around. I had a miniature of whisky left over from Burns night which I sipped at on various occasions, I was quite surprised, however to find that I still had half of it left in the morning.
Trip 140 miles

Sunday 30 January
On rising today the wind had moderated but was still south easterly. The NE trades are somewhat elusive. Some progress was made, but on checking the chart I discovered that the whole days rowing simply returned us to the exact spot we were at two days ago. No orange today sir. Well go on then it is Sunday. Today I nearly ran

into a large cable reel. It would not have damaged the Womble because we go very slowly, but if a fast yacht were to hit it there could be serious damage. Trouble was that it was far too big to lift out of the water and I had no space to put it. There is no one to report it to.

Monday 31 January
Today is the day! Finding north easterly winds when I woke today I leapt between the oars and made hay. The sun shone all day enabling the batteries to charge; we have had thick cloud cover for the last two days. When the boat is lined up with the wind I find that with moderate effort she will make 3 knots, this is new to me, for the last ten days I have been rowing very hard to make 2 knots and on day one I couldn't even get one knot. Three cheers for the north easterly trade winds HIP HIP.....

Thank you all for the text messages, sorry I can't reply, do keep them coming.

Hannah, do you have a name for the teddy you sent me? If so tell my wife (Anita) at the pub and we will have a party for him.
Trip 180 miles

Tuesday 1 February
A wonderful north easterly on waking,, I rowed for an hour before breakfast. Three miles in an hour, unheard of.

Breakfast today was a giant bowl of muesli mixed with freeze dried yoghurt, wild berries and topped with banana chips . Followed by an orange.

Waves.
Waves are generated by wind. They form at right angles to and move at almost the same speed as the wind. If the wind blows from the same direction for long enough, a regular pattern of waves will be produced. The faster the wind and the longer it blows from the same direction, the bigger and more spaced the waves become. With me so far? Good.

What happens next is that the wind, which is self employed and therefore its own boss, changes to blow from a different direction. A new set of waves is produced in exactly the same way. However yesterday's waves are still moving in their original direction, but diminishing in height.

Today's waves are happily waving along when one of yesterday's waves comes slicing through them all at right angles, knocking them in all directions. The wave may not have heard that the wind has changed today, or it might just be a terrorist, but the resulting maelstrom is where the average rower seems to find his or her self. The technical term for all this is a confused sea. It certainly leaves me confused.

Tell me Tompkinson junior, how many miles are there in one day?

Thirty sir

Good man, have an orange

Thank you sir

Wednesday 2 February
Last night a wave found its way into the cabin. It must have been
the aft hatch not secured enough and I woke at two in the morning
to a drenched face and bedding. Worst of all was that Madame
Cholet got soaked as well. She is recovering slowly, but will
probably not forgive me.

Today the sea has been rough, but from the right direction. I have
been able to make some progress, but have had to take a small
break from the sun which has been very strong.

This evening I am listening to Louis Jordan. Earlier I enjoyed
noodles Bolognese and a glass of vino tinto a la Womble.

Trip 242 miles

Thursday 3 February
More north easterlies today, good news and fair progress, the seas
remain high, limiting mileage but no complaints. It seems that I can
get the boat to go at a reasonable pace. I am very happy about that;
I had considered lightening ship, but it would have given me two
dilemmas;

The trip is being conducted in the most environmentally friendly
way and to jettison anything overboard would be inconceivable.
I'm quite fond of my old Chesterfield

I would like to give my many thanks to Doug and Anita Carroll of the Magic Dragon in La Gomera. (It's a yacht, not a pub). They made me most welcome and attended to all of my needs. Thanks you two, see you in November.

I have a gender issue. Does anyone know whether waves are masculine or feminine?

Trip 272 miles

Friday 4 February
A funny sort of day, the conditions ought to have been ideal; light north easterly and patchy sunshine, but I just could not get the boat to go in a straight line and at more than two knots. I don't know, but I'm not going to worry about it.

I had a most enjoyable afternoon listening to New Orleans jazz, then had a call from Tom McCarty and family in Slidell, about 25 miles from downtown NO. The usual crowd of relatives and friends had arrived from Minnessota and all were heading for Mardi Gras.

I'll be there next year boys, no excuses.

After all the excitement I made myself a delicious orange cheesecake.

What have I done?

I ask an innocent question about the gender of waves and wow! So many messages. I am reliably informed by Norman Williams that waves are female unless they are tidal waves, that helps me select a suitable analogy for the next bit.

There is a special type of wave. They occur every half hour or sooner, depending on whether or not you are trying to prepare food or trying to use the toilet or any other task which requires a level platform. The wave is a giant. It resembles a hospital matron at full steam; always preceded by a couple of large bustling sisters and followed by a pair of giggling chanting acolytes. Matron can be seen from a great distance and has a huge white hat. She moves at great speed and nothing gets in her way, including other waves which are simply sucked in and absorbed. Her main job seems to be to encourage the others to keep pace. When your innocent boat gets in the way, it is carried rapidly up her front and up to the hat which is the part that does the humiliating thwack and tosses you and boat to one side for the acolytes to snigger at as they speed along behind. In the time it has taken me to write this we have been hit twice. It must be rounds.

It is two weeks today since I left La Gomera! I think they have been the fastest two weeks of my life. No doubt time will slow down now as life settles into passage routine and I start finding my pace.

Thanks to all who have sent kind messages of encouragement and jokes, keep them coming.

Trip 292 miles

Saturday 5 February
A fine day for rowing and no mistake. After a poor start at 0600 I waited half an hour to see if conditions would improve and I was rewarded. Steady miles and moderate effort.

The gas stove has been difficult to light, but I am getting the hang of it. Last week I thought I might incur repetitive strain injury from the quartz igniter. You just know that your granny would walk in, fire it up with a single click and then look at you as though you were washed up on the last tide. I can now just get it going before the canister of gas runs out.

Tonight I would like to say hello and greetings from the ocean to the Hewett school Norwich and especially to Mr Ian Hawthorn and the year groups I met at assemblies. You were all brilliant audiences and I really enjoyed the mornings I spent with you. A special mention for Mr Walsh's year 11 English class and their guests. Keep up the Hemingway, I'll be back to show you what a real Santiago looks like.

Trip 312

Sunday 6 February

Not such good conditions today I'm afraid, the wind was in the right direction but the sea just did not want to play. I slept very little last night due to a buffeting and so I had my first late lay in of the trip. To date I have rowed the sun up and down each day so I feel guilty about today. Never mind, I can make it up later.

Whilst rowing today I was considering how many of my friends are in the nursing profession and how they might be after my blood for the comparison with the big waves. In my defence I shall say that to my knowledge, the matron is a long extinct feature of our hospitals and although there are political moves afoot to reinstate them, none yet exist, so I could not have been referring to any one person or group.

Anyway it has helped to civilise my relationship with the big waves; when I received a drenching this morning I was able to call out "morning matron" instead of shouting an expletive.

I was talking to my friend Henry Dale yesterday on the subject of hallucinations and I told him about hearing the raucous laugh of an old Alex regular Mary Mc Nally.

Last night I turned on my mp3 player to the sound of "Never mind the ballads" by Norwich band the Last Straw. What should I hear but none other than Mary's distinctive laugh.

My mp3 is a Creative Nomad jukebox with 40gb of space in it. Expertly loaded with thousands of tracks and amusement by Alex front corner sounds man Dave Morgan. Thank you Dave, this system is the biz.

Trip 324

Monday 7 February
With good intentions of rowing I rose at 4 am today to give it a try. Within ten minutes I had to give up. The sea was just too high to row safely in the dark. At 0730 I was rowing. With a short break for breakfast at 1000 I rowed until 1700 for phone hour and dinner. I then rowed until 1940 when I couldn't see any more. I think I rowed about 25 miles, but they were hard fought miles today. The mixed swell made it very difficult to keep on the wind.

At 1830 however, we were visited by dolphins. Thousands of them. They were leaping and playing for about an hour, and they were in every wave as far as the eye could see. I managed to get some of it on film but it was impossible to convey the whole scene. I have been at sea since I was seventeen, this is my eighth Atlantic crossing and I have never seen so many dolphins in one place. The sea was rough and they were loving it.

Trip 350

Tuesday 8 February
At midnight last night a very large matronly body of water hit us and snapped the starboard steering line. The rudder then started whacking around and so I spent some time dangling over the side trying to fix a line to the broken end. I finished at about two and soaking wet climbed into cold soaking bedding. We have had very few opportunities

to dry out over the last few days and with the salt spray leaving crystals every where we are in a somewhat messy state.

At 0800 I tried rowing but it was hopeless. So I stopped for breakfast. I tried again and managed three miles in four hours. At midday matron gave me a bath and washed all of my clothes at the same time. Cue lunch.

Afternoon progress was a little but not much better.

The ocean knows what you are thinking.

I had wondered where all the debris was that is supposed to be floating around, until today. I had seen very little; just a few bits here and there. Well today has been debris day. I spotted hundreds of pale blue sheets of something, probably plastic, about A4 size floating just below the surface. Then I saw a yellow bucket, which I tried to retrieve, but could not row against the win and waves, I then saw what looked like the side of a curtainside lorry and the biggest piece of polystyrene I have yet seen. There have been all manner of things in the sea today, but to my disappointment I was unable to collect any of it.

Thank you for the kind words Liza Perrens and John and Elaine Peck.

Trip 365

Wednesday 9 February
After a frustrating early morning when nothing seemed to go to plan, the day picked up with good rowing conditions. I set myself a target and started rowing. During the afternoon I noticed a drop in performance and took a break. Whilst replenishing my energy stock I checked the hull over the side to find that it is quite badly fouled and needs urgent scraping to give me back some speed. It shall be done as soon as the sea state permits.

Drying out the cabin and Womble warren was possible today with light winds and sunshine. It makes a huge difference to life onboard when the comfort factor is high.

My target for tomorrow is to reach the 23rd parallel by noon. We are now on the trip across the Cape Verde Abyssal Plain, which should take around five weeks. During the transit our heading will be changing gradually from south west to due west, and we should then pick up the north equatorial current to help progress towards Antigua.

Trip 393 miles

Thursday 10 February
Rowing began at 0715 today and was suspended at 0800. An unusable sea, therefore time for breakfast. Soon after resuming rowing it was again stopped, this time for a huge thunderstorm. I'm not sure if there is any danger from the lightning, but to sit at the oars (which are made of carbon fibre, a material which sounds as though it ought to conduct electricity quite well) seems a little foolhardy. If anyone has any science on this please let me know.

Starting the day again at noon, I rowed until 1700 when we reached the 23rd parallel. I am presently holed up in womble warren waiting for a squall to pass before the evening shift.

On reading my weblog I realise that I haven't explained about the oranges. The morning I left La Gomera I went to the farmers market and bought a sack of oranges. I know that there are not enough in the sack to allow me one a day, so I rationed them to one each day that I managed to row 30 miles. They have not been refrigerated and should last a while, however I have had to throw a couple of them away so far, and if they start to go off, I will be feasting on the remainder.

Trip 407

Friday 11 February
Ghastly rowing this morning and early afternoon, it would have been easier to drag the boat over rocks than get any miles on the water, I read last year that some rowers reported rowing "through concrete". I now know exactly what they meant. Better progress this evening, and with the moon beginning to show I might get some night hours in soon.

Friday is Fish day.

We have had dolphin day and debris day, today was the turn of the fish. This morning as I emptied my bowl over the side a Dorado of about 1 metre appeared to check it out. Half an hour later a large fish, gold and black in colour had an altercation with my starboard oar. Later I found that we have been adopted by the Dorado and a number of pretty smaller fish. The bottom of the boat must be scraped asap, or the food chain will complete. The Dorado is quite likely to stay with us for the whole journey, other rowers have told me that they travelled all the way, only to be caught in the Caribbean. There is a picture of a Dorado on the website, it is the blue and silver fish with a stern countenance.

During the video diary today I shaved off my beard. It is a lovely fresh feeling and I recommend it to anyone, even you madam. The beard will have regrown by Antigua, but I intend to arrive in good trim and not like the typical shipwreck victim.

Trip 430

Saturday 12 February
My big plans for today and tomorrow were swept away first thing this morning. I had hoped to row two days at 35 nautical miles per day to get the trip reading over 500 miles, but the ocean doesn't like that sort of thing. I looked out to find less than 100 metres visibility, high seas and increasing wind. Several tries at rowing produced no results and in the afternoon I had to give up completely for the day. At this time (1900 gmt) the wind is blowing 30 knots (force 7) and I am preparing the cabin for the night. The whole boat and anything which has been outside is covered in brown dust, which I suspect to be Saharan sand.

A second Dorado has joined us, I wonder how many we will end up with?

My radar detector has been chirping away merrily today telling me that there are other vessels in the area, but none reply to vhf radio. I call them to ask if they can see me on their radar and to give them my position, but so far, zero contact. It is probable that the bridge watchkeepers are not English speakers.

A very happy birthday for tomorrow to my nephew David Delaney of Hull, have a great day buddy.

Trip 447

Sunday 13 February
Last night at about 1130 a huge wave hit us and snapped the port steering wire, washed everything loose all over the deck, filled the footwell and took away a pair of my socks which were out to dry. I put out the sea anchor, lashed the rudder and left everything until this morning. I spent some time sorting out the mess and fixing a new steering line and finally got rowing at noon. The wind has shifted to the North and the temperature has risen by five degrees. I can use a northerly for a little while, but I could really do with some north easterlies to take me over the abyssal plain.

The Dorado have an amazing skill. They were play fighting today and their colours changed completely from the blue, yellow silver to a fierce looking black and yellow, which is what I saw the other day when my oar was attacked. It was the same fish after all. They are such good hunters and have such a turn of speed that I am becoming unsure of whether or not to get into the water with them, we shall see if my bottle holds up.

Trip 473.

3 clicks to light the stove tonight

Monday 14 February
Another write-off day. The wind has shifted again, this time to the North West, a direction which is definitely not required thank you. I

17

spent the day trying to get some west or even just south into the direction but no chance. At least it has been sunny and warm and I managed to dry out just about everything.

My pal Norman, a resident of Tenerife, tells me that it has been colder there than for the last fifty years. That explains a lot to me. I have been suffering from the cold in the mornings to the point where I have been wearing three layers of clothing until 10 or so each day. It has been a real chore to leave wonderfully warm womble warren in cosy cabin to go to cryogenic cockpit and bare backside to builder's basics black bucket. Most rowers reported that it could get cool in the evenings, but I was not ready for UK temperatures.

Two more Dorado joined us today, one is bigger than all the others and has a slightly different shape of head. They attacked the first shoal of flying fish we have encountered. It looked like a shower of silver foil over a wave, then I realised what they were and the Dorado were there in an instant but they would not have had much of a meal from them, they were very small.

For dinner tonight I had Mexican chicken with rice and olives, (delicious) followed by strawberry cream cheese, (yuk).

Trip 485

Tuesday 15 February
During the night we were blown backwards four miles, which I have not been able to recover today, so the sea anchor goes out tonight. This is a shame, because there is a northerly component to the wind, which is useful.

A glorious day however and I tried rowing in my birthday suit for the first time. I enjoyed the feeling and will probably do it again but not as many rowers do, ie row naked the whole journey. Why? Well there is a certain amount of chafe in delicate areas and it is still so very cold when the sun is down.

This evening I shaved my head. I now look like the captain of the starship enterprise.

How to tidy the cabin of an ocean rowing boat.

First get into the cabin and sit down facing forward.

Then pick up each item on the starboard side of the cabin in turn, examine it closely, consider it and then deposit it thoughtfully on the port side.

When there are no items left on the starboard side, brush the crumbs, toenails, bits of freeze dried food, dead skin fragments, salt crystals from the mattresses into the snake pit just inside the hatch and resolve to clean it out later.

Then take all of the items on the port side of the cabin in turn, examine etc. until the port side of the cabin can be brushed down. Divide the articles between the two sides of the cabin and hey presto, spring cleaning complete.

The oranges are going rotten now, so I'm eating them as soon as possible, I'd rather not ditch them.

Trip 493

Wednesday 16 February
Happy birthday Mum

Happy 25th wedding anniversary Neet.

Today was just great. Not many miles, but all in the right direction for a change and a good morale boost. Several Wilson's petrels sighted today and a tuna has joined the Dorado as escort to this mighty ship.

We sit presently on the sea anchor (the big boy) so that the miles we earned today are not taken back, and a party atmosphere prevails with the drinking of champagne and the conspicuous consumption of a grand banquet in celebration of our wedding anniversary. The wombles are astonished that we are having yet another party but they can rest now until the half way point when the fridge comes in handy for champagne again.

I swam under the boat today to scrape off the fouling which has occurred during the last month, it was fairly well distributed and easy to remove. The Dorado did not give me any trouble, but I did pick my moment carefully; they had gone off somewhere to get some grub (probably Sainsbury's) because they don't get anything from me.

I have been asked to tell you all how to contact me. You can send a free text message via the Iridium website, you need to use my satphone number which is 00881631570778.

Due to a glitch between my phone and computer I cannot exchange e mails with anyone or reply to text messages, but if you send an e mail to my normal address, my wife will read it out to me.

When sending text messages, if you do not send me your name it will be anonymous. I don't mind either way. You are limited to 160 characters or so, but you can send more than one message. I turn on the phone for calls between 8 and 9pm GMT daily, but please remember to call from a landline or you will be hit with massive charges.

This bulletin is sent in honour of the front corner of the Alex pub and all of the erudite sages therein. Buy yourselves a beer chaps, cheers.

Trip 503

5 clicks

Thursday 17 February
After four hours of rowing side on to the wind today I decided that enough was sufficient and altered course to go South. I need some Southerly miles yet and there is no point just sitting around waiting for the wind to go in your favour. I was rewarded with good conditions and an enjoyable row. The boat speed has increased about half a knot after the removal of the fouling, so it is worth doing.

I called the Unthank Arms in Norwich this evening, a fundraising wine tasting and quiz was being held for the Davenport trust. It was so good to hear everyone enjoying the evening , so much that I took a glass of red myself to get into the spirit of the occasion.

A fantastic night sky tonight. We are five hundred miles from the nearest light pollution and the view simply doesn't get much better than this.

Dinner tonight was delicious pasta primavera.

Trip 520

5 clicks

Friday 18 February
A pleasingly productive day!

I began rowing at 0700 and with two short meal breaks rowed until 1900 with near perfect conditions. More please, just like that. The wind is due to shift more to the east tonight which is exactly what I need. Keen observers of my position will have noticed that I am heading for the Cape Verde Islands. Over the next couple of weeks my track should move more westerly as I leave the Canary current and head for the North equatorial.

I have discovered why the trip readings which I give here are not tallying with the ORS figures. The GPS onboard does not read any speed less than 0.9 knots, but the trip uses the GPS to calculate the ground covered. Quite a bit of my journey is at speeds of less than 0.9 knots so the trip reading is lower than it should be. The ORS track my movement with Argos beacons which have a better GPS than mine, so you can rely on their numbers.

Trip ish 540

1 click yahoo!

Saturday 19 February
Upon waking this morning I spotted a ship on the horizon. On checking, I found that he was on a steady bearing from me, which means that we were going to collide. I took to the oars and rowed west for ten minutes until his bearing began to move left. He answered the vhf on my second call and said that he could see me on his radar; that is good news, it means my active radar transponder is working. The forecast wind change happened on schedule and the easterly wind is now of great assistance and very welcome.

My daily mileage should begin to improve soon as the winds become more consistent.

The last orange was eaten today.

If you mix dried milk powder with sea water it tastes really odd.

Today was jazz day.

Trip 561

7 clicks

Sunday 20 February
Today was spent recovering the four miles that we lost last night when the wind blew us North. Some Westerly headway was also made, so a reasonable day, but very little to report except for a spectacular Dorado fight at about 1500 this afternoon. A huge eruption on the surface about 20 metres from the boat. They had all changed colour and were in yellow and black. I wonder if they were establishing terms with a newcomer. There are at least a dozen of them there now.

Since the trip reading is now proven to be meaningless I have decided to include it anyway.

Trip 561

12 clicks

Monday 21 February

A very sunny and hot day, with steady but light winds, good rowing but for some reason the boat just would not go above 1.5 knots. I was informed that Maud Fauntenoy, who is rowing in the Pacific, has covered 96 miles in the last 24 hours. Gadzooks, if you have any miles to spare Maud......

Tonights celebration is for one calendar month at sea, and by my calculation, about a quarter of the way to Antigua. Ending the shift an hour early to watch sunset with a glass of red seemed like a good idea.

To celebrate further I brought out a new sheepskin for my cushion. The difference is striking. Comfort levels improved at a stroke.

Yesterday I spotted a huge piece of polystyrene at about 500 metres. It was about the size of a large fridge and I decided that it would be our first decent piece of recovered debris. The plan was to row upwind, get East of it and drift down on the wind. This was all planned like a military manoeuvre, including the method of embarkation and the eventual stowage. We reached the upwind point earlier than I imagined we would and drifted down to the polluting article. The ocean can give your eyes some odd perspectives to deal with; our fridge sized block was the size of a housebrick and very easy to embark and stow.

Trip 588

1 click

Tuesday 22 February

Happy birthday my youngest brother Andrew

I think I must have upset someone. Today the sea was fine, the winds were in my favour but still, the maximum speed I could get from the boat was 1.5 knots. I tried different techniques but to no avail. I tried the scrape the oars along the top of the water as if you were curling butter method; 1.5 knots. I tried the dig deep, heave until your knuckles part, your legs creak in compression and your blood tries to force its way out of your forehead method; 1.5 knots. I just cannot envisage what it would take to push a rowing boat 96 miles in one day, that must be some buzz.

The forecast for tonight and tomorrow confirms my suspicion that I am in someone's bad books; the wind is to come round to the south, or west, or both. Dust off the big boy.

This evening has to be the calmest, warmest and most agreeable of the trip so far. I sat in the cockpit for dinner (chicken teriyaki, yum) and the silence was complete. No sound of any kind at all. The night sky was only slightly impaired by the huge full moon. I looked over the side to see our squadron of Dorado which now numbers about thirty, cruising in a lazy moonlit clockwise circle beneath us. I rowed for a while in the silence, but decided that I was making too much noise and returned to the cockpit to just sit and appreciate. It is beyond me to imagine Norwich in the snow right now.

Trip 601

3 clicks

Wednesday 23 February
As forecast, at 3am the wind arrived and it was a fifteen knot south westerly. Out big boy and have a lay in.

This morning I got on with some maintenance. I removed the rudder and cleaned off the fouling, checking the shackles and fixings whilst there. I cleaned out the watermaker compartment, superglued my kettle handle back on, cleaned out the fridge and cooker, baled out the bilge pump locker, cleaned my pans etc etc. All this takes my mind off the fact that we are on the sea anchor and not making any progress, especially westerly progress.

During the afternoon I called customer services. Yes, hello, this is a south westerly and I'm going to Antigua; it should be a north easterly. Little, l i t t l e. No I don't have my booking reference number with me. Antigua, A n t i g u a. Yes about three months ago. North easterly, Yes, about force five or six. Yes I'll hold. Music. Hello, yes, I see, so when will my winds be delivered? When? Is there nothing you can do? I've been waiting five weeks. No thanks, I don't feel much like completing customer satisfaction surveys just now. Goodbye.

It seems they mixed up my winds with someone else who was sailing and she got the north easterly. She didn't want hers either. Ellen somebody or other.

The wind increased during the evening and I couldn't use the cooker, so it was cold corned beef hash tonight, which is not as bad as it sounds.

Trip still 601

No clicks, no cooking

Thursday 24 February
The wind veered slightly this morning to just north of west, so I recovered the sea anchor and gave rowing a try. The only direction I could make was just west of south and only one knot. However I

reminded myself that one mile is better than no miles so I plodded on for the course of the day.

The temperature is increasing slightly in the mornings. I'm so glad, I was wondering if I would be wearing three layers all the way. Sad to hear that Norwich has so much snow. It's funny, when I'm listening to my blues records some days I just think of the Walnut Tree Shades with the tables outside and the sun beating down. I can almost taste those whisky sours. Set one up for me Chris.

I was reading through my diary yesterday and came across the entry for the maiden voyage of the Womble. It was on Sunday 18 July last year and we launched from the Woods End at Bramerton. The crew were Andrew Vinsen, ocean rower from the Woodvale race 2003, and James Downey, promising rower, and myself. We shared the rowing, (when Jim would let us) went to Coldham Hall, had lunch, and rowed back. We all enjoyed the day, but got soaked to the skin in the rain. Rowing, eating, getting wet. That about sums it up.

This afternoon I became convinced that the ocean can read your mind. I was rowing along thinking that I haven't seen any whales this trip when I heard a snort on my left. I saw a small whale about 4 metres long with a curved dorsal fin well aft on its back The fin was rounded at the end. It was very inquisitive and made several approaches. Then there was two. They swam around for a while until I got the camera out and then disappeared, not however until I got a pic or two. Half an hour later a repeat performance, but since I didn't have time to become well acquainted with the first two I could not tell if these were new observers or simply the last ones coming for a second look. It always gladdens my heart when I see the beasties of the sea, they are so elegant and confident and at home in the water, which is just as well really.

I saw a great shearwater today.

Trip 608

12 clicks

Friday 25 February
Happy 60th Birthday Roger Cawdron.

Mixed fortunes today with the wind, we had a westerly for all of the morning and I tried several times to get some use from it, but in the end I had to concede and did a food inventory instead. I made some discoveries;

Three jars of peanut butter tightly wrapped in duck tape to prevent breakage. These were inherited from last year's race and were in a container I had left in La Gomera. Also in said box were 5 kilos of good muesli, some tinned food and all of the gas I need for my stove. All very useful, but the peanut butter is a valuable treat.

Three packs of olives

Two jars mayonnaise

1 jar Almogrote

1 malt loaf

It doesn't sound much but these goodies will go a long way. Almogrote is a delicious paste from the Canaries which is made from parmesan cheese, garlic, red peppers and vegetable oil. I intend to try making it myself when I return.

At 1500 a faint breeze began to blow, from the East! The oars were immediately started and I rowed until 2000, when the breeze died away.

The forecast for the next few days is dire, but I intend to see if it becomes true before I get gloomy about it, these things are not really reliable.

Thank you Scottish Courage for the kind message today and thanks to everyone who sends me texts, they are all very welcome and keep me a troshin.

Trip 617

Nine clicks

Saturday 26 February
This morning was another beauty, the sea was glass, there was not a breath of wind and again a stunning silence. I began rowing and enjoyed the stillness for most of the day. The sea is still smooth this evening so I hope for a good nights sleep.

Last night I dined on freeze dried lasagne with meat sauce. I could not believe how good it was. So, I hear you ask, how many of these priceless gems do you have onboard? Well actually that was the only one. Due to time restraints I was unable to adequately source and sample the full range of freeze dried foods available, so my range is somewhat limited.

My second favourite food is curry. So, how many curries do you have onboard Tiny? Thirty? Forty? Fifty? Well actually it's zero. Yes a big fat zero. I could list many foods that would have been easy to buy and stow onboard and which would have been very welcome, but for some reason were omitted. However, that is the way it happened and I shall have to look forward to my goodies at home.

ORS trip 704

My trip 629

3 clicks

Scallops

Sunday 27 February
The wind woke me at 1 am, 15 knots of wretched westerly, big boy
deployed. Ho hum. I keep telling myself sooner or later this must
change, but it keeps looking like later. We are now 150 or so miles
north of the westernmost Cape Verde islands and on the
springboard of the crossing itself. I just want to get cracking.

  I keep seeing large tankers and bulk carriers so I must exercise
vigilance at night, they come within a couple of miles so they are a
significant danger. Once I am clear of the islands and the main
shipping routes the traffic should thin out and I will sleep easier.
The main problem with the ships is the bow wave. To be struck
square on by the ship itself would be unlikely, but the bow wave will
overturn a rowing boat very easily. Ask Sam Knight. (ORS Regatta
2004)

This morning breakfast was scrambled eggs, bacon, beans and
coffee.

Trip 631

Three clicks

Monday 28 February
We drifted backwards again last night, that made us five miles east of our Saturday night position. I began rowing, but could not make any way against the westerly wind, so the sea anchor went out again. I spent the morning cleaning out the snake pit and the bear pit, shifting weight from forward to aft and doing some laundry. At noon a bulk carrier came within half a mile, so as he approached I recovered the sea anchor and began rowing. I was able to make about one knot with the wind at ninety degrees, very awkward but I managed to regain a lost mile or two. At 1500 I was exhausted and took a small siesta on the sea anchor. By 1600 I had lost a mile again, so began rowing. At 1845 I put out the sea anchor and called it a day. Still two miles behind Saturday.

Dinner was a scrummy long grain and wild rice pilaf, from Mountain House. With it came a sachet of parmesan cheese and I noticed that it was made by Sargento foods Inc of number one Persnickety Place, Plymouth, Wisconsin. I love names like Persnickety so if any of you live in a place with an unusual name, please let me know and I'll give it a mention.

Norman the clicks number at the end of my bulletins refers to the number of times I have to squeeze the quartz igniter in order to fire up my recalcitrant gas stove. Funny you should mention it today.

Trip 642

43 clicks

A Little Goes a Long Way

Tuesday 1 March

At 1100 this morning the awful truth dawned; we are in the grips of an eddy or a countercurrent. I rowed from 0800 until 0930 when I had to break for a while to do a job, during which I put out the sea anchor. By 1100 we had been taken east two miles. There was very little wind, so it must be current. I have rowed all day until now, 2100 and I intend to row on and off through the night and tomorrow to try to get us away from it. The forecast is very light winds, so we should be able to make about 1.2 knots. I measured the current to be 0.7 knots.

The elements have certainly done whatever they wished to me, I wonder when it might be something of use?

The temperature continues to increase and I wear fewer clothes, the mornings are now quite bearable, and this evening I am able to row wearing only a t shirt. Have no fear madam; it is very dark.

This evening when scraping out my bowl and washing my spoon a Dorado leapt up and bit the spoon. It must have looked like a fish to him. I wondered where they had all gone yesterday, until I dragged in the sea anchor and they all sheepishly followed it back.

Thank you for your message Scrannon and Anne, please tell his nibs greetings from the ocean, and congratulations on his wedding plans; I only heard today.

Trip 652

16 clicks

Wednesday 2 March

Last night I rowed ferociously until midnight and managed to clear the eddy. I noticed the boat speed increase to 1.9 knots by 2300 and guessed that we were clear; another hour for safety and we were done. It was calm during the night but we even managed to drift half a mile west and two miles north. This morning however everything changed again and a 20 knot south westerly has been keeping us on the sea anchor all day and has taken back at least three of last nights hard won miles. I have no comment.

I spent the day very constructively looking for Wally in one of the books my daughters gave me. Wally is a stripey character who carries a pile of books and is fiendishly difficult to find among the hundreds of people and goings-on in a large double page drawing. The drawings themselves are entertaining enough with different themes and a vast amount of detail, but once you have found Wally you must then find some of his friends and pieces of their kit. You may have gathered that this book is for children, and you will need photo ID at bookshops in order to buy it, but it keeps me amused for ages; by the time I have found the third or fourth person or item, I have forgotten where Wally is and I have to start again.

I'd like to dedicate tonight's bulletin to the Welsh quarter in the Alex, I hope you had a good birthday Fizz, and thank you all for keeping my daily positions updated.

No clicks, too rough to cook.
Trip 656

Thursday 3 March

Last night was mayhem; high seas, the boat being flung about and the rudder crashing from side to side. It was too rough to have any hatches open and I slept very little. Today I decide to try something different. The forecast is that these westerlies will become north easterlies by Saturday, so with the prospect of two more nights on the big boy, I removed the rudder and cast out all the remaining rope, which secures the big boy to the boat. Result; The rudder noise has gone and the boat rides much more steadily up and over the waves because she points more to windward. Jackpot. Now why didn't I think of that weeks ago?

I have become all excited about Saturday, three different forecasters agree that the trades will return and I shall be on my way. I plotted the rest of the journey on my routing chart and I need to go west for 100 miles to reach the optimum current for the passage to Antigua. If I get this right, the second part of the trip should be much quicker than hitherto.

Tomorrow then, will be big preps day, greasing seat runners, getting snacks and drinks stashed, consuming calories, scraping the barnacles from the hull and charging various batteries. It will be like setting off all over again, I wonder if the Dorado and dolphins will wave me off? I feel rooted to the spot here.

My music system continues to keep me happy, but one of the speakers on deck has gone duff, so I can only listen with one ear. There is something a little unreal about singing womble songs at the top of your voice into an empty ocean. Environmental health will be round soon.

I am advised that Matrons do exist in the modern world, and that I may be asked to account for myself to members of the Royal College of Nursing. I know enough about nursing to be aware that you don't mess with the RCN. Gosh.

Today's bird was a Cory's shearwater, and I think the Great
Shearwater I saw the other day may well have been a Cory's.
Today's came closer and was better identified.

I'm taking this as a good omen too – 1 click

Trip 659.

Friday 4 March

As today progressed my excitement grew. The wind shifted slowly
around through north at noon, to north-north east at 1600 and at
1800 we had north east, so I brought in the sea anchor to see what
would happen. I had replaced the rudder earlier and we were ready
to go. The boat began to drift west at 1.3 knots. First class. Let's
row!

This afternoon a plane came over, circled a few times and left
towards the south. I caught a curiously familiar glimpse of good
quality silver gleaming from the cabin. This brought on a feeling of
deja vue which stayed with me for some time.

Four dolphins came by earlier today, but showed no interest in the
boat, just passing through. The underneath of the boat is now a
mobile aquarium, with hundreds of small stripey fish. There is one
fish which I particularly like; it doesn't glide around like the
Dorado, but seems to fly like a slow moving sparrow. It is about a
foot long and has puckered lips as though made for cleaning the
bottoms of boats. Perhaps it has been sent by a well-wisher, but as
yet the goose barnacles continue to grow and need scraping
regularly.

Today, breakfast was a grand bowl of special muesli with yoghurt, wild berries, dates, dried apricots and banana chips. Coffee, no newspapers.

Happy weekend everyone.

Nine clicks

Trip 668

Saturday 5 March
My excitement yesterday was well founded, this morning the wind was still in the north, but soon veered eastwards and by noon was north east, 10 knots. As the day progressed our speed crept up until late this afternoon we were bowling along at 2.7 knots. Let's hope it stays until Christmas.

The radar detector has been sounding all day, but no sign of any ships, it starts off with just a short beep now and then, and gets louder and more regular as the ship approaches. It was screeching like a mynah bird today, but it must have been a stealth ship. The detector is called a Sea me and is made by Munro engineering. I bought it second hand and when I had problems wiring it in I called Munro. I explained that it was not new and the gentleman very patiently helped me through the problem, and all this on a Saturday morning. If only more companies could be bothered to offer that level of customer care. www.sea-me.co.uk

A potentially serious problem occurred this morning at 0945, just after the Womble song and during a spoof State of the Nation address by GW Bush esq; the remaining speaker on the music system fell silent. The snag might be fixable, but I must face the possibility that the rest of the journey could be somewhat quiet. My short wave radio took a wave onboard a few days ago and has not been heard from since, so no world service. What next?

Tonight's bulletin is dedicated to Mr David (Errol) Flynn and his colleagues from Waverley vintners and Gallo wines, who very kindly supplied the bacchanalian stocks held onboard. Thank you gentlemen, your astonishing good health.

Three clicks

Trip 681

Sunday 6 March
Happy Mothers day Mums everywhere, and you Mum.

This morning the wind was from the East, and about 15 to 20 knots. Perfect. I began making miles but during the afternoon I ran short of steam. Sitting around on the sea anchor for so long has softened me up somewhat, but in a few days I should be back up to fitness. An exciting navigational moment today; we entered the box grid on my routeing chart which takes us through the westbound stages all the way to Antigua. There are seven boxes to transit, each one a mental milestone.

Today was definitely for the flying critters. I spotted two new Petrels, a British storm petrel and a soft plumage petrel. We were also visited by two types of Shearwater, but I haven't got a definite ID on them. Centre stage today though were the first two squadrons of full size flying fish. I have only ever seen these from the deck of a large ship, and I always had the impression that they just made it out of the water and skimmed about. From my best seat in the house at the greatest show on Earth, I can report that they fly well clear of the water achieving heights of maybe twenty feet and are very agile and aerobatic. No doubt I shall witness even more spectacular flights from them but today's was a good starter. The Dorado are meant to prey on these fish, but ours didn't seem to notice them. I wonder if they haven't seen them before?

On the subject of Dorado, it is becoming more likely that I will have to supplement my diet with fish, as the food stocks onboard might not last me all the way. I will give the situation consideration over the next two weeks.

The text messages you continue to send me are very welcome, thank you all for your kind words.

Thank you Mrs Trellis, but I'm not sure that Earlham Road qualifies as a funny place name.

Henster, thanks bud, all's tickety boo in the B and B departments. Thanks Matt and Ali, I'll give it a try.
One click

Trip 724

Monday 7 March
Happy birthday Kevin Bainbridge.

Good rowing conditions today, but probably not the best mileage made, a bitty sort of day when I couldn't quite get the boat 'on the step'. Some days are just like that.

The ocean looks different every day. No two days are alike, and it just feels like a different place every day. It's a bit like driving through countryside, the features are similar, but not in quite the same place. Not much in the way of wildlife today, but one of the bigger Dorado did a massive leap this afternoon. They usually do a second leap, and I hope to catch one on film.

The good news so far today is that after good advice from Matt Boreham I dried out my short wave radio and it is back to normal (difficult to tune, will not stay on station and the alarm won't switch off. Also world service mostly inaudible). Thanks Matt and Ali. Matt rowed in the ORS regatta last year and his wife Alison is to take part in the ladies fours boat in the Woodvale/ORS race in November this year.

More good news, this time for all of you who spend time looking for biros. You know who you are, you strongly suspect that a biro collector is in your employ, or it was that greasy rep that visited the other day. Well I now know that they really do slip in to another dimension.

There were three biros onboard when we left Gomera. No one has been on the boat but me. No biros remain. I can account for one, which both ran out and fell apart simultaneously. The designer deserves credit for that; no wasted effort in manufacturing there. This means that the remaining two are somewhere else in the universe or in another universe altogether. There could be a whole planet dedicated to biros. Well anyway you don't need to look for them any more, they just ain't there. Go out and buy another.

Thank you so much Denise, Geraldine, Barbara, Honour, Roberta and Larry for your kind greetings. You were the last people I saw and I am looking forward very much to seeing you all again and I will be delighted to hear you sing the Womble song in the pub. The offer of soap opera updates I will pass on thanks, but if you wish to send text messages (free) see the instructions in my diary entry for 16 February.

Tim Welford (former Royal Marine and ocean rower) of the Blue Boar in Poole asks if my beer will last; Tim I don't have a drop. You couldn't arrange a Hercules could you?

7 clicks

The trip reading is so far out by now it is not even worth mentioning. I will give a different figure; the nautical miles to go to Antigua - 2055nm

Wednesday 9 March
I keep thinking it's Saturday.

The beard shears came out again today, I was amazed at how quickly it had grown. Maybe my increased metabolism is the cause, my nails seem to be growing faster too.

The wind has vanished, likewise any current that might have been around and the sea turned to depleted uranium; jolly hard to row through. A very hot day also and one which should have been spent in the shade on licensed premises in an exotic location.

During last night I rowed for four hours to try to make up some miles, but it wasn't productive enough to warrant the effort and lose the sleep. I had some interesting hallucinations; first I heard a loud crack like a gunshot out to the port forward side, later I felt something gently prod my back whilst rowing. Fascinating stuff. How does the brain conjure up all this nonsense?

Whilst rowing I saw a fair number of commercial aircraft fly over, I must be under the usual route between Europe and South America. Once clear of this corridor I guess the next route I see will be into the Caribbean. We are now clear of the shipping lanes which skirt the Cape Verde Archipelago, so the sea me has gone quiet. Peace.

A change of oars was decided upon today with the medium weight Excels being retired in favour of the super light Bracas. It is too early to tell if they will be all rounders or just for certain sea states, but they certainly feel a lot less effort to wield than the Excels or Suttons. The Suttons were my favourites when training, but the gearing is a little heavy out here.

Greetings today to the staff and students of Framingham Earl high School in Norfolk, thank you all for making the Womble and myself so welcome in December, I hope you will allow me back to tell you how the trip went. Thanks also to Mr Mike Sanderson for arranging the event.

Six clicks

To Antigua   2025nm.

Thursday 10 March
What a cracking day! We began with the gloomy news that we had again been blown backwards during the night, but only by three miles or so. However as dawn broke the wind suddenly changed and began picking up from the north east. The lost miles were soon

regained and we bounced merrily along all day at speeds of 2.5 knots plus.

My latitude is now where I wish to be, and my longitude is now my prime concern. A small amount of southerly leeway can be tolerated, but going west is the main objective. Antigua lies at approximately 17 degrees north and 62 degrees west. We are less than 100 miles north of the Antigua latitude, but 2000 miles from its longitude. I am navigating with care along a line on an Admiralty routing chart which shows a favourable current from here all the way into Antigua, but by now we all know how reliable the trade wind and currents are! I am barley twisting my fingers as I type.

There has been one of those giant swells today, the tops are at least half a mile apart, maybe a mile, and the whole ocean seems to tip as they pass through. It resembles driving through the Cotswolds, but you don't drive over the hills, they lift you gently up and pass underneath you. Very soothing. When you are at the top of one of these aquatic hills you can see great distances, which would be useful were there anything to see.

The music is sadly no more. The speakers on deck are not for resuscitation and I have no earphones. The short wave radio is now my sole source of music, and it is fair to say that there isn't a great deal of my kind of stuff to be had. Never mind, I shall just sing.

Kenneth Crutchlow of the Ocean Rowing Society tells me that we have been featured on the Explorers Web, a large site based in New York. We extend a warm welcome to anyone visiting from that site. Please feel free to contact us with any questions or observations you may have.

If any of you live, or have lived in places with unusual or funny names, such as Persnickety place, then I would like to hear from you. Send a free text message via the iridium.com website to phone number 0088 1631 570778. If you tell me your name I will assume that you don't mind me mentioning it in my diary. You can (and you do) send anonymous messages.

7 clicks

To Antigua 1999 nm

Friday 11 March
Another good rowing day, but off to a slow start. The wind was from the north this morning and was presenting big seas, to which I was rowing at right angles, very difficult and uncomfortable. Early in the afternoon the wind veered and conditions improved instantly. I rowed continuously until dark, when the wind backed to the north! The journey feels as if it has commenced properly now that we are heading straight for Antigua.

My new oars are proving very useful, during the beam seas today I realised that due to the gearing the handles have a good gap between them at the centre of the stroke and when I catch a bad wave I do not have my shins stripped of skin and the bones crushed.

So that's nice.

Day 50. Can you believe that I have been messing about in the Atlantic for seven weeks now?

Dorado

These fish are becoming the prevailing theme of this diary, but I must tell you what has happened.

We had about thirty of them swimming under the boat until a couple of days ago when we crossed 25 degrees west. The numbers are down to about a dozen (twelve, kids) and they all seem to have grown much larger. Either they have been eating each other, or they operate a territorial patrol system. It would be a bit like London cabs "Sorry guv, don't go south of the river" The fish version would be "west of 25? Not me pal, that's big boys country over there"

Hello this evening to listeners of BBC Radio Norfolk, with particular greetings to Glenda, who provided me with my Wombles sheet, and Alan, who provided my Wombles duvet and pillowcase. They are in regular use and most comfortable thank you.

Thruster! Great to hear from you and thank you for your greetings, we must have a beer on my return.

Dave B of Worcester, no I'm not wearing a comic relief red nose as I row today, but a sunburned real life version. The kiosk was closed on my way down this morning. If anyone cares to bring a collecting tin tonight you can have all the cash onboard, which comes to 14.70.

Hello Louis and Ellie, thank you for your thoughts, I'm thinking of you too.

Seven clicks

To Antigua 1965nm

Saturday 12 March

A bouncy night last night and the first time that I felt that we might capsize. On two occasions the boat went so far over when thwacked by large waves that it just felt as though we were upside down. This boat and others of the same design are incredibly robust and stable. Any other boat would have rolled over last night. The designer deserves a tribute for his or her achievement on this. Provided certain conditions are met, these boats also self-right if they capsize completely. They must have the metacentric height of the Eiffel tower!

Yesterday's mileage was a bit more like it, I need to get a whole lot more like that; about ten weeks worth. Today's will not be as handsome as yesterday's, the wind and sea have been fully beam on and I struggled to keep the speed up.

I'm starting to hanker for various things, some of which I would never normally eat. Today I felt as though a large quantity of toffee would have been welcome.

My muesli is running out, mixing it with just about anything is making it go further, but it will be gone by Tuesday. It is a rather good blend of jumbo oats, wheat flakes, barley flakes, raisins, apricots, roast peanuts, sultanas, dates, sunflower seeds and brazils. If you mix it with freeze dried yoghurt and wild berry dessert it is simply scrumptious. It is exclusive to the Daily Bread Cooperative in Cambridge who put people before profit, and quite right too.

Thank you for your message Jess, there is a picture of a Dorado somewhere on the wall in the pub.

18 clicks (it got wet last night)

To Antigua 1939nm

Sunday 13 March
A beam sea again today, but very little wind. The current seems to
be doing its work well, when combined with a breeze it gives me the
best part of one knot, which is a fine advantage compared with the
head winds and eddy currents of two weeks ago.

The loss of my music is hurting, the rowing sessions would go by
very quickly when listening to, among many others, Albert Cooper,
the Last Straw, Louis Jordan, The Zutons, David Bowie, Howlin Wolf
and of course the Wombles. In addition the machine held
"Forgotten Voices", a number of first hand accounts from survivors
of the First World War, which I particularly enjoyed, and my
linguaphone Russian course.

My weight continues to fall; I estimate that I have now lost two
stones or about twelve kilos. The food onboard is sufficient for
another ten weeks, which should see me into Antigua, but I shall
probably lose quite a bit more weight yet.

Why should a Sunday feel like a Sunday out here? There is a definite
feel about particular days of the week and it has followed me to a
place where it really has no relevance. Answers on a postcard please.

21 clicks

To Antigua 1911nm

Monday 14 March
A gloomy typical mundane Monday morning. Heavy cloud cover,
cold wind, stiff joints and a slow start. Midday brought bright
sunshine and lifted spirits.

This evening you were to be addressed with a sad lament of the boat being blown too far south and off the magic carpet current putting us into the eddy zone and so on until tears came creeping out from the corners of your eyes.

The going had become decidedly tough during the day, with a maximum speed of 1.7 knots from vigorous effort. At 1600 during a stand up and get the blood circulating break I took a look over the side to see if my favourite fish was there. A black line about six feet below the surface stretched across my field of view. Bewildered, I was about to poke an oar down to try hooking it up when it suddenly dawned on me that what I was looking at was the sea anchor rope. The rope is 100 metres long and it sinks, so I had two 50 metre lengths of rope looped at the bottom and they were being towed wherever we went.

Once the rope was back into its bucket I began rowing and easily made over 2 knots.

Each evening before retiring to my stateroom I perform deck rounds to spot just that sort of problem, I must have been half asleep last night. Tomorrow, in order to determine my fate, a court martial will be convened.

The muesli will last another day, maybe two.

Six clicks

To Antigua 1879

Tuesday 15 March
Happy birthday my dear chum Jacky.

Jolly fine rowing weather. The happiness factor is rising onboard, largely due to our progress and the party coming up on Thursday. Distance wise, we will be one third of the way to Antigua by noon. This milestone has been a long time coming, if the winds and current remain as they are the next ones should pass more speedily.

After my court martial this morning I began rowing and took a break for lunch at 1300. The cooker would not light. No gas was getting through and it seems totally blocked. Searching the boat for the destructions took too long and I didn't find them anyway, so for the moment the freeze dried food is being rehydrated with cold water.

How did what go?
Oh the court martial.

Court Martial Convened.
Call Captain James Little

Sir.
You are charged the on the 14th of March you were negligent when carrying out deck rounds. How do you plead?

Guilty sir.

You put me in a very awkward position Captain, I have to be President of the Court, prosecutor, defending counsel and defendant.

Sir
It's a good job you have pleaded guilty, that makes things much easier. This is a very serious matter though. Have you anything to say in mitigation?

I must have been very tired sir.

No excuse, guilty as charged then, I sentence you to be relieved of your command, you will take your vessel to the island of Antigua. Sir.

Carry on.

Thanks for the messages David and Alison Kirk, Ian and Bev, Guy Arnott and Dave Bennett.

The only photos I have are still in the once-only cameras I am carrying and will be developed in Antigua. I will post the best of them on the site as soon as I can.

A big hello from the ocean to all listeners of Radio Broadland 102.

No cooker, no clicks

To Antigua 1845nm

Wednesday 16 March
This morning the wind had shifted to the south east, which is not disastrous, but not the best. Soon after I began rowing it died altogether, so progress has been a bit slower today. Fine sunny weather though and a happy mood onboard.

Yesterday I spotted a piece of debris, which I thought might be collectable, so I rowed back to have a look. On arrival it turned out to be a large sheet of a type of composite wood, which was too large to lift. Underneath the sheet swam hundreds of the species of fish to which my little favourite under the boat belongs. I know not yet whether she has stayed with them or has continued her odyssey with us.

With the help of the ORS forum contributors I have managed to fix the cooker. It was un petit morceau de soi dans le carburetteur. Many thanks to all concerned. It is good to have a reservoir of experience to call on and very reassuring.

Fixing the cooker cost me a few miles today, so please forgive me a short bulletin, I have an evening shift to row.

One click – of course

To Antigua 1823

Thursday 17 March
Happy Saint Patrick's Day

Today's goal was to reach 30 degrees west. That was achieved at 1714, and signified that we are now one third of the distance through our journey. Yippee.

During today's row I spotted several of my favourite fish (whatever they are) close to the boat and it seems that Myrtle (for that is her real name) has brought her chums along for the ride. What an honour.

Whilst drinking your Guinness this evening, you are permitted to have a derisory chortle at a chump who forgot what would be happening in his absence and failed to include a few tins in his shopping list.

The last of the muesli was consumed with relish this morning. I now face a challenge to prepare daily breakfast with whatever is available. I shall keep you informed.

This evening, in recognition of the milestone we passed earlier, a gargantuan gastronomic extravaganza will be served in the long room. Carriages at 3am.

1 click

To Antigua 1804nm

Friday 18 March
Have an absolutely spiffing week end everyone.

Another fine day and apparently a fabulous day in Norwich too. Soon be summer. My pal Norman tells me that the crocuses are out in Chapelfield.

The sea me has been active all day, but no visible ships. This must be traffic between Brazil and the Mediterranean.

My latitude is now only forty miles North of the Antigua latitude, so I need to level out my course and head due West. It feels like we are swinging onto the home straight, but with a mere 1780 miles to go.

Some time ago I told of hallucinations involving a prod on my back. No hallucination. During deck rounds yesterday, which were carried out with diligence, zeal and sobriety, I discovered the corpse of a small flying fish which had its nose bent over. This was close to my rowing position and must have been what I felt.

Breakfast this morning was a crushed and disintegrated raspberry jam flapjack with dates, dried apricots, banana chips and whole milk. Jolly tasty it was too. The flapjack, and a whole lot more like it, were donated to me by Paul of Paul's News in Rosary road. Paul and his staff run a very fine shop and post office and I am very grateful for the gift.

Thank you for your messages Frank and Daphne, Fran and Pete, Tim-thanks for the Dorado recipes, and Gary.

Three clicks (oh oh)

To Antigua 1780nm

Saturday 19 March
Congratulations Wales on winning the grand slam at six nations rugby.

The Atlantic rowing club must have had a sign outside this morning stating that no boat shall exceed 1.3 knots today, for that was that maximum, whatever the conditions or amount of effort expended. There was not one cloud in the sky for the whole of today. The sun rose as I rowed, roasted me slowly for the whole day and set as I rowed. Just another day.

The result of the Wales game was broadcast on the world service this evening. They also broadcast the match, and I tuned in, but as soon as the match started the reception faded to the usual level; inaudible. Radio Sweden is well heard out here, also radio China in as many languages as you care to learn, radio New Zealand, radio Moscow and just about any station on the planet. The BBC world service though, is hidden so well that you need the trained ear of an asdic operator to pick it out. This morning I enjoyed listening to radio Portugal. My Portuguese is not brilliant, but they broadcast some home grown folk music, which I enjoyed very much, especially the bit that goes da da da da dum dum da.

Chicken teryaki for dinner tonight, followed by vanilla and raspberry dessert, both scrum yum.

One click

To Antigua 1759nm

Sunday 20 March
A most excellent day. Rowing began at 0700 and finished at 2000 with a few short breaks. The sign outside the club has gone, so boat speed today was over two knots and the miles clocked up regularly. Occasionally a cloud gave cool relief from the relentless rays and all was very happy on the Womble.

An interesting event at noon; a 50 000 ton bulk carrier appeared without warning about a quarter of a mile away and heading straight towards us. A short period of intense activity followed and he passed us by at very close quarters a few moments later. The boat had been manoeuvred to take his bow wave and all went well. My VHF calls went unanswered and no one came out from the bridge. Perhaps the bridge was not manned.

The ships name was Onde and was Japanese. No teryaki for me tonight.

My invertor has been playing up. What's that? Well, it converts my solar powered battery bank voltage (12 volts) into mains voltage so that I can power the laptop upon which I type these bulletins, one of the VHF radios relies on it, also my moribund music system and the video camera which I use for filming events of note. A few days ago I was trying to resurrect my music when I discovered that the invertor simply would not work. I stripped it out, checked everything was ok and tried again, but still nothing. Two hours later it started working normally. Intermittent faults are always the hardest to fix, so my confidence in the machine is not high.

Thank you for your greetings Barbara, Jacky, Andrew, Henster, Matt and brother Steve.

11 clicks

To Antigua 1728nm

Monday 21 March
Today began much the same as yesterday and by noon we were bouncing along merrily knocking off the miles. It is so exhilarating when the current and wind are in your favour and the boat speed starts to rise. Such a shame then when you are cracking on and everything goes awry. It started with just one darkish cloud from which a light shower emanated. The sea beneath became boisterous and confused, and soon there were more clouds. By 1600 the whole area was a messy maelstrom and rowing was very difficult. Still we managed to meet our mileage target by dusk and as I type we are drifting west at one knot or so. In the morning I shall row from 0700 until 1000 to top up today's mileage, and then we begin again. Too much detail? Ok.

Scadzoodles of flying fish today, they seem to leave the water simultaneously in numbers of about thirty, do a few aerobatics and re enter as one. A large splash near the re entry point means that the Dorado had secret intelligence and knew where to loiter. An adult flyer was found dead on deck yesterday morning and it made at least one of the keel squadron happy.

Today's yearning was for a bowl of peas on Reggies stall in Norwich market. By the time you read this it will probably be Wednesday which is specials night at the Earlham house tandoori. Vegetable curry mmmm, I shall be there in spirit.

Thank you for the kind words Chris and Maureen, Sally and Sarah, Wendy and Steve. Norm you will be pleased to know that I am smiling.

Seven clicks

To Antigua 1690

Tuesday 22 March
Squally and difficult rowing, eventually I became weary of drenchings and gymnastics, so I spent some time tidying and calorie cramming ready for the settled conditions. The music system was also tinkered with but no cure yet.

Some of you may have spent time in your youth with a transistor radio under the bedclothes at night listening to radio Caroline or trying to listen to radio Luxembourg (Reception was about the same as the BBC World service). Those of a certain vintage will recall that it was illegal to tune into Caroline (it was a pirate station moored off the coast of Essex.) Between the two stations was the whole range of the music that teenagers and some parents wanted to hear, but until the arrival of radio 1, we were denied. My uncle Lol bought me a transistor for passing my 11 plus, and it was late at night and in secret that I did my listening. Well anyway, I turned on this very laptop a couple of days ago and noticed a very faint chime as it fired up. I searched vainly for the speaker, then tried to play some music on it anyway. To my great delight it worked, albeit as faint as faint can be.

In order that in the evenings I can re enact my youth and straining my ears, listen to my favourites, I have begun transferring music from my mp3 player onto the laptop. The only snag is that the laptop battery lasts about an hour; the invertor must then be run to charge it. The invertor makes enough noise to drown out the music. Nevertheless it is a fine piece of progress. Hurrah.

Speaking of progress, we are now on latitude for Antigua, yet it seems inevitable that we will drift further south yet, but in the 1600 miles or so left to go west we should be able to tidy up the course. Two Cory's shearwaters and several Wilson's storm petrels sighted in the last few days.

Tonights bulletin is dedicated to our supporters and sponsors in the lounge bar in the Alex, fine folk you all are.

Two clicks

To Antigua   1658

Wednesday 23 March
Today began well with a brisk north easterly wind and a well regulated sea. Rowing was good, but not as fast as Monday. At 0900 the wind veered east and stayed there until 1500 when it backed to the north east. It has now moderated to a slight breeze.

Whilst rowing today I felt a few spots of water on my head and face, and looked up expecting to see a cloud. Two flying fish whizzed by one meter above my head.

Without the music to numb my mind whilst at the oars, I have begun recalling places, names of friends and acquaintances, events, just about anything which has happened to me during my life. Most of it seems like a comedy, my laughter must be audible for some miles. Over the next few days I shall endeavour to remember something legal, credible and printable as an example for you.

Today's lunch was a half packet of freeze dried scrambles eggs, fried with a good quantity of sliced salami. Exquisite. My forthcoming book "Single burner banqueting" will include such delicacies.

My wristwatch came alive today to tell me "enjoy your exercise" Hmmmm.

Three clicks

To Antigua 1617nm

Thursday 24 March
Not a bad day, the wind and current have been kind, and I was able to take a couple of hours off during the day to attend to cabin matters. The mattresses and bedding have been covered in salt crystals from the wind and various soakings when airing on deck, so I took each item in turn and first brushed off the covers then sponged off any remaining salt. The salt is itchy, a bit like loft insulation but also gives a greasy feel to fabrics.

The washing machine was then brought into action for the duvet cover and some other laundry. Everything dried very quickly so we have a fresh feel to the warren tonight.

Two pairs of birds arrived today, white with black streaky heads and very long tails. Possibly white tailed tropic birds but I'm not sure yet. I think one is called Keith. Well that's what the others were calling.

It is nine weeks tomorrow since our departure, if present progress can be maintained another eight weeks should see us just about there. My daily routine has changed as the journey has passed; it will no doubt be fine tuned until arrival.

Six clicks

To Antigua 1585

Friday 25 March
Happy Easter

Slow rowing today with an unusual sea state which made things a bit corkscrewy. We are being taken south, which is not brilliant, but I expect that we will have the opportunity to regain our latitude later. Maximum boat speed today was 1.8 knots.

The yoghurt covered raisins ran out today, and I thought we had run out of tea, but I found some more tea bags in the galley locker.

The sea me has gone quiet, we must be off the beaten track again. The next shipping lane is between New York, Recife and Rio de Janeiro.

Thanks for your messages Ali, good luck in the marathon.

Cheers Henry, if only I had paid more attention in the history class.

One click

To Antigua 1556

Saturday 26 March
Falling asleep whilst typing my diary entry last night tells me that
my new routine is making the most of my energy reserves. The
daily mileage is presently good, but is due to favourable conditions,
which may not last. If the wind and current go against me again I
will be furious with myself for not making miles now.

Matron came by this morning, picked us up like a rugby ball and
ran for a hundred metres before touching us down.

Mr G. Glass of Morecambe sent me a free text message via the
iridium.com website to my phone number 0088 1631 570778, to
ask me what sort of engine I have fitted in the Womble

The engine presently in use seemed at first to be an unlikely
candidate for the job. For a good number of years it had been
assigned to light duties only. No maintenance had been carried out
on it and an advanced state of decay was evident. Despite all of this
it was regularly in steam, no more so than annually at the Royal
Norfolk Show when a full head of steam was always achieved.
I took the engine to David Cosford at the University of East Anglia
to see if he had any ideas. After a number of preliminary checks he
proposed an extensive programme of testing and a full schedule of
exhaustive trials. The boiler was of prime concern, its VO 2 max

was determined and a full pressure test performed to see if its total aerobic capacity was sufficient.

The firebox, main cylinder, piston, crankshaft, governor and connecting rods were all examined, cleaned and replaced. Crankshaft deflections were less than one thousandth of an inch. All bearings were checked for hysteresis and the lub oil was replaced with a fresh batch for low cholesterol, high haemoglobin and good haematocrit. The main support columns were tested along with their universal joints and despite a slight difference in length were deemed acceptable. The flywheel was removed and a large amount of mass removed from it – mostly rust. The spark arrester and sootblower were removed and scrapped as they would no longer be required with modern fuels.

The tests revealed that the plant, although very old and in poor condition externally was basically sound.

The trials schedule involved hot ops, cold ops, and power range testing to determine its lactate curves and draw up a boundary of operation table. One hundred hours of fine tuning on an ergometer were then carried out.

At this stage the fuels consultant was appointed; it was vital to feed the boiler with the correct balance of high efficiency fuel to ensure that a full head of steam would always be available.

The trials were deemed successful and the propulsion unit was put to work on the boat. Despite some steep gradients, the unit has performed adequately to date.

The engine is of course my own body, and David Cosford is the assistant Director of Human Performance at the University of East

Anglia Sportspark. The fuels consultant is none other than Anna Suckling of NutriTactics, an expert sports nutritionalist. I am very grateful to both of them for their support and assistance in the preparation for this project.

Thank you all for your continuing text messages, they are priceless to me.

Two clicks

To Antigua 1523

Easter Sunday 27 March
Happy birthday George Glass

Today was a moderate activity day; rowing for less hours and carrying out personal maintenance. Breakfast was a raspberry flapjack with a raspberry and apple porridge mix. Lunch was chicken and herb dumplings and dinner my fave pasta primavera with blueberry cheesecake for pudding. Parts of me which I have never seen before have begun to appear, so I must still be losing weight. A few more days like today should help.

It appears that since the arrival of Maud Fauntenoy in Tahiti , I am the world's only ocean rower in transit. Wow. Should I feel lonely or something?

By my calculations we should reach the half way point sometime late this week. The ORS hospitality ship should be on station now, and I look forward to our rendezvous. You know, the ship with the wet dock at the stern; you just row into the dock and the boat is taken over by white uniformed sailors who give you a big fluffy bathrobe to wear into the shower area. Kenneth and Tatiana

Crutchlow are waiting on the verandah deck dressed in immaculate tuxedo and ball gown. They are smiling and holding cocktails. Your boat will be cleaned and replenished whilst you sleep soundly. In the morning your steward will bring you ice cold orange juice, a handsome cooked breakfast with freshly ground coffee. Careful with that paintwork boys.

The ocean wildlife seems to have gone quiet. The Dorado are still here, the flying fish and that's all. The distance from the mainland must be the reason.

Today's bulletin is dedicated to Reverend Nick Gerrard , Curate Damon and the parishioners of Saint Thomas' church, Earlham Road Norwich. We are in proud possession of the blessing Nick performed for us on the 13 December on the river Wensum in Norwich. Thank you and happy Easter.

One click

To Antigua 1497nm

Monday 28 March
This morning rowing began at 0715 and proceeded jolly well until 1000, when I stopped to bring the log up to date. Ten minutes later I took the oars to find that we had run into a gluey clag of water, which stayed with us all day and restricted boat speed to 1.4 knots. My belief that we had left all that nonsense behind was ill founded.

The news of another Indonesian earthquake reached me today. A couple of text messages have asked what I will do if a tsunami hits us. The short answer is that I will probably not even notice it. The water depth here is over 4000 meters and the likely wave height would be only a few feet or less. It's when the wave reaches shallow water that it gains height due to the funnel effect. We regularly experience huge swells, which usually come from the north and they pass through without incident. How they begin and where they end up is a mystery to me.

A tropic bird early this morning, another this afternoon, one cory's shearwater and another shearwater yet to be identified. Some beasty or other, probably a turtle, has been munching the bottom of the boat at night. It could be eating the goose barnacles, which must have re grown by now. If so it gets my vote.

The banana chips ran out today, also the penultimate jar of coffee.

Thank you tonight to Colin Blackburn and his pals from Redcar Dave and Derek. Also thanks to Hilary Bastone of the ORS and Jon Lacey of Prestige Gardens.

One click

To Antigua 1470

Tuesday 29 March
The detention register at my former school, assuming they have kept it, will show that I was once given a detention by a praeposter, (which is a similar creature to a prefect, but they get to wear sawn off academic gowns), for "persistence". The prae was a chap called Kim Button, who went on to be a policeman. My recollection of the incident is sparse, but I do remember wondering why I was being punished for something that I thought was a virtue.

Persistence paid off today, the conditions for rowing were dreadful all morning and most of the afternoon, with maximum boat speed of 0.9 knots early, rising to 1.3 knots. Normally I would have found something else to do, but today I kept trying to get more until at last, at about 1700, something happened (I don't know what), and the boat speed suddenly went to 2.5 knots. With the few hours of daylight left the mileage became acceptable in the circumstances.

Kim Button's career was, I hope, long and successful, but I wonder how many villains he marched into the station with charge sheets reading "patience", "perseverance", "diligence" and the like.

One of the seat roller bearings seized solid earlier, it took me a while to get it replaced, but oh was it worth it. The seat now whispers back and forth instead of the rattle and graunch we had before. Peace.

Thank you Andrew and Wendy for the messages, also Matt, that will be fine on Thursday.

Four clicks

To Antigua 1452

Wednesday 30 March
The rowing conditions today were almost identical to yesterdays, with a meagre mileage and too much sitting around waiting. No problem, there is always some job or other to do.

This morning my number one Argos beacon stopped sending my position, so I was telephoned to arrange to switch on number two. The beacon sends my gps position to Argos, who are in France, who then send my track to the ORS There is an emergency button on it should I have difficulties, also a well man button which I would press daily if we suffered a communications breakdown. The batteries in the beacons last for ninety days, which is why we carry two. This one has lasted seventy days, but it might not be battery failure.

My court martial has been troubling me, I think I was harshly treated, so I have been thinking about grounds to appeal. There are a couple of angles I could go for, so watch this space.

My obsession with food continues; I counted the food packages again today to be sure that we have enough to get all the way. It looks about right, so long as we get steady miles. I have never been hungry before and I don't particularly relish the prospect.

Tonight we have a common tern onboard, but it is finding it difficult to stay as the boat is presently moving around violently.

Thank you Guy Arnott, the log may well be included in a book, but I have some work to do on the rest yet.

One click

To Antigua 1426

Thursday 31 March
Big seas this morning, but quite rowable so I gave it a try. Ten minutes after I began I felt a strange sensation in the very centre of my lap, if you know what I mean. A small flying fish had landed in a delicate place and was trying to make good its escape. With a bit of help he was gone, but the experience was yet another new one for me. The sea stayed big and bouncy all day, but I found that with

effort we could head slightly north of west, which helps us regain some miles lost to the northerly winds of the last few days.

The invertor seems to have recovered, it was required to run a soldering iron today when I fixed the telephone charging lead and it gave no trouble. Phew.

KT asks what do you need electricity for on a rowing boat? Good question, when I rewired the boat I was surprised at how many outlets I needed for the switchboard, and it is easier to list them:-

GPS, (global positioning system)
VHF radio
Navigation light
Water pump
Battery charger
Compass lights
Cabin lights
Music system
Invertor (drives spare VHF, movie camera, computer, anything mains voltage)
Satellite phone
Fridge
Cellular phone
Radar detector
Water maker

Some boats have bilge pumps, wind instruments and more, so it is quite a list. When ocean rowing started there was hardly any of this kit, they took all of the water they needed, all their food and set off with no phone or safety beacon, just themselves. To me they were the real heroes. Intrepid adventurers.

Thanks tonight to Sam in Oz, Guy Arnott, Jo Edye, Jacky , David Cosford and staff at the UEA Sportspark.

Seventeen clicks

To Antigua 1404nm

Friday 1 April

The months seem to go by quickly out here, it seems only a short time since the 1st of February. Today was one of those difficult rowing days when the maximum boat speed is governed by someone else. At one point I was applying great effort to achieve one knot.

We did, however manage to crab a few miles towards our goal without going any further south so that is a good sign. In the weeks to come I will be taking every opportunity to make a few northerly miles. The prevailing winds here are north easterly and rarely blow from the south east.

With progress being so slow I decided to clock off early and had a luxurious shower in the sunshine. My beard was removed again and I now feel fresh and clean. Well about as fresh and clean as ocean rowers get. To anyone else I probably smell ghastly.

My hand held GPS has been re programmed with a more accurate waypoint for Antigua so you will notice a difference just for tonight in the miles to go figure; it will look as if I have gone even fewer miles than I really have.

The geographical half way point should be reached sometime on Sunday, I plan a small celebration onboard.

One click

To Antigua 1400 (see above, distance run was more like 20 miles.)

Saturday 2 April
The wind obligingly veered to the East this morning making rowing a good deal easier than yesterday. We made some good miles and as I type we are only two miles from the half way line. We should drift over tonight.

Clouds

Every navigator needs to be aware of the weather and a good indicator of what is about to happen is in the message of the clouds. Clouds can tell us a great deal about what is happening in the atmosphere above us. They can herald the arrival of a depression, or perhaps a more local event such as a squall.

Red sky at night, shepherd's delight means that the clouds are breaking up from the west, and are colourfully illuminated, showing that a trough of low pressure is moving away to the east. High pressure is likely to follow. Red sky in the morning, shepherd's warning means that well lit high clouds are increasing from the west and are indicators of an approaching depression.

Clouds are named according to their shape. A lumpy cloud is a cumulus, thin feathery clouds are cirrus. Flat clouds are stratus and raining clouds are nimbus. These names are often combined eg stratocumulus and cumulonimbus.

Over open ocean the clouds tend to form streets, or if a posh area avenues. These well defined features can extend for hundreds of miles out here in the trade winds. The stronger winds tend to be found between the avenues. A good skipper will cast his eyes heavenwards each morning to carry out a forecast for the day. Looking at the clouds so far this trip, I have seen; bunny wabbit, chuffa twain, angel, thwan, duck, dicky bird, nuther bunny wabbit………

Thanks Fraser, you had me laughing out loud.
Cheers Arfa and Pauline in sunny Scunny.

 Three clicks

To Antigua   1371

Sunday 3 April

Hello, good evening and welcome to the very first outdoor broadcast
of my daily diary. The evening is so calm and warm that it seems
silly to be in the cabin.

If you had been here at midnight last night you would have seen
me, cold coffee in hand looking out to sea. What was I looking for?
The half way line of course! We drifted quietly over the line shortly
after the hour and I was so excited I couldn't sleep.

Why was I drinking cold coffee? The next thing which will run short
is cooking gas, so I have placed a ban on hot drinks. When I mixed
the coffee cold I was pleasantly surprised so I tried the same with
tea; also very good. Since I have only seventeen tea bags left I
suppose it doesn't really matter.

In the cellar I have three large bottles of lime cordial. They were
supposed to be for the second half of the trip, but a small sample
was taken last week. Today however they are legal for consumption
and I intend to use them in a rationed manner for drinks and for
cooking. Tonight I will prepare cheesecake with lime. Earlier I
opened a packet of olives, drained the brine and drizzled them with
lime. My menus will be checked carefully to see if lime can be
added to anything. Obsessive, me?

Today was to have been a take it easy and party day, but when I rose it was clear that this was a goood rowing day, so the banyan was postponed and I did a full day's row. Remembering the days when the boat will not move at more than one knot keeps me keen when conditions are right.

A half bottle of champagne had been in the fridge all day and has been a welcome sundowner this evening. Thanks Paul.

My nephew Peter Delaney has promised me a CD autographed by all of his band if I mention them here; this I am proud to do so let's hear it for Soundcraft of Hull. I earnestly look forward to attending a summer performance.

Today we have received very many calls and messages from you all congratulating us on the milestone. Thank you all so much, it is gratifying to know that you are keeping an eye on us.

No clicks yet

To Antigua 1343

Monday 4 April
Another fabulous evening so we are outdoors again.
As the sun rose here today I found myself submerged in five thousand meters of water cleaning a Womble's bottom. The scouts give out badges to wear for skills like that. If such a badge exists, I would like to wear it.

When I rose today it was obvious to me that it was flat, flat calm; I had not been pummelled whilst trying to sleep and my breakfast did not try to escape. A first try a rowing produced slow results so I decided that since it was calm it would be a good idea to scrub the bottom of the boat. It was quite heavily fouled and my first effort with the fish slice cleaned most of the barnacles away. The fish did not seem bothered, so I swam away from the boat some way and took a photograph. The rowing speed increased by about 1 knot. By lunchtime the heat of the sun had been intense for long enough so I ventured over again to finish the job with sharp scraper and pan scrub. Success and another quarter knot.

The rest of the day was enjoyable, if a touch warm and we notched up our miles steadily.

This afternoon three oh-so-common terns arrived and sat on the front of the boat. Expecting problems, I ceased rowing and made ready to evict them. Sure enough within a couple of minutes there was a fight and I had to break it up. They flew off to make trouble with a dark petrel, but he soon got the better of them and back they came. A second and third round of evictions took place before they got the message. They will probably return.

Two clicks.

To Antigua 1311

Tuesday 5 April
Those dreadfully common Terns did not return, I think we gave them the slip. Good thing too.

The temperature today was over 40c during the afternoon, which made rowing uncomfortable. It is now 1730 and no sign of any cooling off, so my intention is to take a long break now and row into the night. Last night was good for rowing; I had five miles left to do so I started again at 2200, finishing after midnight. A warm and pleasant row with a spectacular sky. Cosmic.

The clean hull is giving us a good turn of speed, it will be interesting to see our performance when the trade winds return.

The shortwave radio is not particularly cheery at the moment, I wonder when we might be able to receive some Caribbean music. We could have a calypso party onboard. Ah, but we have no rum. 2030 It's all gone wrong. A small siesta was being taken after typing the last paragraph, but I was wakened by wind. Bad wind. Northwesterly bad wind and now we are on the sea anchor. Well I never.

Hopefully this wind will veer and we will be on our way.

My court martial was, in my view unsatisfactory and an appeal will be heard on Friday.

No clicks yet.

To Antigua   1290

Wednesday 6 April
At 2200 last night the wind moderated enough for me to begin rowing, so the big boy was recovered and we set off. An hour later came a veer, which sorted everything neatly out and I retired to bed. This morning the wind had not changed and was reasonable, so I rowed all day in sunny and breezy happiness until 2100 this evening.

In about two hours we will drift over 40 degrees west, which is one of my milestones, the next one will be 1000 miles left to row.

The day before leaving   *Photograph Elaine Peck*

Preparations in
La Gomera

75

Departure   *Photograph Pete Dawson*

Outbound   *Photograph Pete Dawson*

Half way

Curious Dolphin

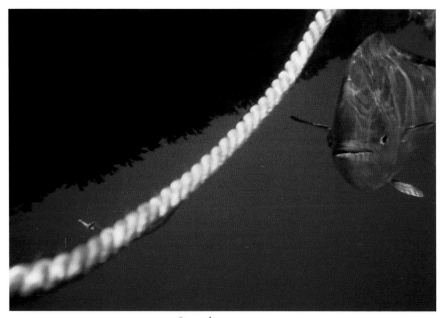

One of my escorts

A tangled sea anchor after a rough night

Cosy Cabin

I see him, but he can't see me.

Arriving in Nelsons Dockyard, Antigua. *Photograph Ted Martin*

Womble rests in Antigua

Last few yards

First beer

It doesn't matter how you arrive, formalities must be done.

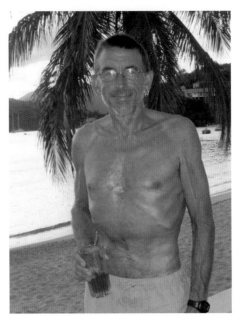

Ten days after arrival and fattening up nicely

Someone asked me today to define a veer. The wind is said to veer when the direction from which it is blowing moves around the compass in a clockwise direction. The opposite is when the wind is said to back, when the direction moves in an anticlockwise direction.

Listening to radio Canada international, I heard that the BBC is to cut its broadcasting on short wave. I have to ask the question; how will we know?

Thank you Glenn and Samina, I hope we will be over to see you later in the year.
Thank you Nigel and Paul in HK.

Three clicks

To Antigua 1256nm

Thursday 7 April
Last night at midnight or so we drifted into an eddy, from which I am still trying to extricate us. These eddies are quite difficult; there is no way of knowing where you are in them or how wide or long they are. This particular eddy is moving at about one knot in a northerly direction. That may not be too inconvenient, but it knocks a big lump from our top speed. On the charts the currents are shown either as a straight line or a wiggly one. This gives the false impression that the whole body of water is moving in one direction at a fixed speed. The real nature of the current could be represented by spaghetti strewn along its track, with an indication of the net flow written somewhere nearby. (If you must try this at home, first cook then cool the spaghetti and dab it dry with a tea towel. Put clingfilm over the chart. When the illustration is over,

make up some Bolognese sauce and some almogrote. Delicious. Don't forget a glass of Chianti). Snakes and ladders is the game that springs to mind.

An apology
Sorry everyone, but I think I made one of my paragraphs in the bulletin of 27 March a little too realistic; I have been sent many messages asking how the rendezvous went. There is not, nor has there ever been a hospitality ship at the half way point. These journeys are made with no assistance or support and I am not allowed to accept anything from any other vessel. The ORS ship I spoke of was a figment of my imagination, a mirage, a myth, a fantasy. Many apparitions have presented themselves before me on this trip, it was just another.

I'm quite nervous about my appeal tomorrow.

Two clicks

To Antigua   1237

Friday 8 April
Freeing us from the eddy took until this afternoon. An hour of rowing last night showed that there was nothing I could do until morning, so I began rowing west at 0600 today, with a maximum speed of 0.9 knots. The speed crept agonisingly slowly until quite suddenly at 1630, it went from 1.8 knots to over 3 knots, and eventually 3.4 knots, a record for the trip so far. No more of those, thank you.

The world service has been loud and clear today, did someone have a word on my behalf?

Court Martial Convened

Court convened for an appeal.

Call Captain James Little
Sir

Well, Captain we are in an awkward position again

Yes Sir

You wish to appeal against your sentence?

Sir I believe I was in possession of unsound advice when I entered a plea of guilty.

But as your defence counsel I gave you that advice

Quite so sir, but I believe you may have been as tired as I.

So you wish to change your plea to what?

Not guilty sir

Very well, explain yourself.

Sir when I discovered the rope it was in the water on the starboard side of the ship.

Yes
Well sir, when I carried out deck rounds the evening before, I would not necessarily look over into the water for anything as part of my rounds, I would be looking only for things not correct on deck.

Yes.

That night was to turn out to be a rough one, and it is entirely possible, or even probable that the rope was in its correct position when rounds were carried out, and was cast over during the night. But as it was a correct item, rather than an incorrect one, it would not have made an impact on my tired consciousness. That, I submit sir, makes my conviction unsound.

Yes I see, do you wish to call any witnesses?

There are no possible witnesses sir, which I believe reinforces my case.

CCTV coverage?

No sir

Very well, I have heard enough, Captain and I'm of the opinion that your conviction is not safe and your appeal is allowed.

Thank you sir

Afterwards

Well done Captain, that's cleared up nicely. Aren't you due promotion soon?

Yes sir.

Well I should think you will have something in the post soon. Drink sir?

Well just a quick one.

Phew I'm glad that's over.

Happy week end everyone.

Thanks again Fraser

One click

To Antigua 1209

Saturday 9 April
This morning I began rowing at 0615 and realised immediately
that we were enjoying the assistance of the current. It seems
quite rare that the wind and current both line up exactly with the
direction in which we wish to row. The effect is dramatic.
Normally I would have to put considerable effort in to get the
boat over two point five knots, today we were travelling at 3.4
knots for at least two hours with very little effort. During the day
that speed dropped slowly off as the current meandered off to see
its pals somewhere, but it was very welcome and can come by to
visit any time.

The BBC world service was completely impossible to find today, I
wonder what goes on there. That's one day of clear reception in
seventy eight days. Maybe they put an extra shilling in the meter
for the Pope's funeral yesterday and the number crunchers have
shut them down for the day.

The present forecast for arrival in Antigua, everything permitting,
fingers crossed, is the middle of May. To achieve this I need to row
33 nautical miles per day. It is possible, but very much subject to
lots of variables, so please do not rely on this as a forecast. I will be

unable to pin my arrival date down with any accuracy at all until Antigua is practically in sight.

Three gas cylinders to go, they last twelve days normal usage, that gives me gas until 6 May, but without hot drinks it might last all the way. Exciting isn't it?

Thank you for your messages Jeff, and thank you for getting the diary entries to Aunties Brenda, Glad and Louie. Please give them all my love. No sign of the teapot lid.

Jacky the clicks are how many times it takes me to light the gas cooker, I was going to drop the feature, but can you believe someone is having a sweepstake on it!

Wendy, no I'm not building muscles, just getting skinnier.

One click

To Antigua 1169nm

Sunday 10 April
Happy birthday Sheila

My steward knocked gently on the headboard this morning as he brought my coffee.

"Will you be rowing today sir?"*

As I replied in the affirmative the boat started moving at one knot. When I rose and left the cabin a half knot was added to our speed. As I sat on the rowing seat another half knot. Picking up the oars and dipping them gently into the ocean, another half knot, and moving the oars oh so gently took our speed up to three knots. As the sun rose our speed crept up and steadied at 3.4 knots, where it remained all day.

We seem to get on so well that I do hope the current becomes a regular visitor.

A ship appeared on the horizon today, a container carrier of some size. No reply on VHF radio and he was gone. It was my intention to warn him about our bow wave. The sea me chirped merrily for a while last night, but I saw nothing when I checked.

Flapjack for breakfast today, lunch was pork casserole and dinner, smokey bacon mash and peas, then wild berry yoghurt for pudding. Who could ask for more?

Is there a technical term for someone who talks to themselves? If there is, I have joined their ranks. This afternoon I realised that I was announcing the plan of the next couple of hours aloud, as if to a crew. The sooner we get to Antigua the better.

Tonight's bulletin is dedicated to our wonderful bar manager Sheila, who is celebrating her birthday today.

* Before the text messages start coming in, I do not have a steward, I am rowing solo, on my own, by myself and have no one with me. I make joke.

One click

To Antigua   1119nm

Monday 11 April
Happy birthday Amanda at the Bramerton Woods End, 40 today.

Whizzing along all day at three knots again. An exhilarating row and a few more miles under the belt. The current has taken on a northwesterly set at about 1.75 knots. Thirty miles of that is useful, but we need to head west only after that please.

The Dorado have not had a mention for a while. Any flying fish which land on deck during the night are collected and donated to the first fish to realise that I am offering them. Today it was the turn of the biggest of them, a leviathan of 1.5 meters and weighing probably as much as me. He made his approach to the handful of fish and then turned away and left them to be scoffed by one of the others. How did he get that big?

The squadron currently number about fifty and make an eerie sight when swimming beside the boat in the dark. They look silver when the moon is up. During the day they all go off in pursuit of flying fish and are exceedingly fierce predators; a successful catch is an impressive sight. They can leap twenty feet out of the water and often do it seemingly for fun.

The rice puddings ran out yesterday, the dried apricots and dates will be next. No matter, we shall have less than 1000 miles to go in a couple of days and as the miles disappear into our wake such luxuries will become irrelevant.

Thank you all for your continued messages and greetings, Ben your message did get through first time.

No clicks yet

To Antigua 1072nm

Tuesday 12 April
Great conditions again today, a little bouncy here and there, but good miles and not too hot with about 50% cloud cover. A twelve hour shift today yielded thirty six miles, and the boat is currently (pun intended) heading west at 1.9 knots!

Our next event is the passing of the 1000 miles to go mark, which will be tomorrow morning. A lime cheesecake to celebrate I think. Onboard my next small event is the turning of the chart. My Atlantic chart was far too big for the cabin, so I cut out the section containing the journey and folded it in half so that it would fit into a waterproof wallet. The wallet is opaque on one side, so in two or three days I will have to take it out and lo, there shall we see Antigua. Small things can appear big out here.

Radio Norfolk called this morning for a chat, I hope you all got up early to tune in the wireless. The pace of conversation took me a bit by surprise, it all seemed very quick and I wonder if I have slowed down or whether I was just a bit yawny. The latter I hope, I was slow enough to begin with.

Seven clicks

To Antigua 1019

Wednesday 13 April
Hot hot hot today, very little cloud cover and I got a roasting. Summer is coming in these latitudes and over the next four weeks I will probably have to spend more time rowing at night and

sheltering during the day. Slightly fewer miles today I expect, the current has not been in line with the wind, which has been strong. My routine has evolved as the trip has progressed, it is mostly to do with the time zone change, but the net effect is that my rowing day has extended from ten hours at first to fifteen hours now. More than fifteen hours would, I think affect the quality of work, so the last few weeks will not change further.

As expected, we crossed the 1000 miles to go line at 0730 this morning, and we have just passed 45 degrees west. Next milestone is two thirds of the way there in a couple of days.

Guy Arnott asks me if I have come across any big debris such as floating containers, and he informs me that there are over 250 000 of the things out here somewhere. Guy, no I haven't, but early on I did go through an area of concentrated debris which coud have come from a shipwreck. There is a website run by someone called Ebbsmeyer which deals with this stuff, I'll try to get the address for you.

Tonight's bulletin is dedicated to Colin and Marge at the Fat Cat real ale emporium in Norwich. They are project sponsors, for which I am deeply grateful, and they are raising funds for the Davenport trust whilst I am rowing.

Four clicks

To Antigua   965

Thursday 14 April
This morning I confidently mounted the rowing seat, made myself comfortable, unclipped the oars and boldly ordered "warp factor 4 Mr

Sulu". Mr Sulu pressed some buttons and immediately Scotty's voice piped up "We've got no warp drive captain, the dilithium crystals have had it". So we had only impulse drive and only factor 5 at that.

The current has vanished, and the sea is a confused mess so we can make only 2.3 knots. Just as I finished rowing tonight I thought the current might be returning, but the morning will tell. If it has gone for good I shall miss it, the feeling of skimming the tops of the waves with the GPS reading four knots is one that will stay with me. Today though, back to the troughs in the sea and steady effort. The wind and sea have become very lively tonight, so I expect very little sleep.

During today we had a spot of rain, but we passed close by a thundery looking storm cell which reminded me of a similar event earlier in the trip. It made me wonder what happens to a boat if lightning decides to stop by. Onboard we have a copy of the Atlantic crossing guide by Gavin McLaren and Anne Hammick. ISBN 0-7136-6075-9. It is an excellent book with good port information and masses of useful facts. Here is what it says about lightning; "The effects of a lightning strike are likely to be severe.There is a distinct possibility of structural damage – aluminium mastheads can be melted or split, and if the charge leaves through a skin fitting it may be destroyed. If it exits via an encapsulated keel, then a section of the GRP may be blown off. It is likely that most of the electronic equipment onboard will be destroyed, whether powered by ships power or batteries, and whether in use at the time or isolated. The damage may be obvious – in some cases instruments will virtually explode or be blown from their mountings........." It goes on to say that the vessel should have a full survey as soon as possible and that the engine and gearbox may also be damaged. It says that even the astro navigator's digital watch will be destroyed. That should wipe away any smugness.

"Surprisingly, injuries to the crew are rare" That's the bit I like, but what about those carbon fibre oars?

Two clicks

To Antigua   927

Friday 15 April
Twelve weeks at sea today.

As expected, sleep was a rarity last night; the wind was up and still is. We have had a similar day to yesterday, and we are still on impulse drive only. However at one point in the afternoon I detected some current, so it is still here somewhere. If only ocean currents were in colour.

We passed the two thirds of the way mark today, but the big one for me was turning over the chart. Antigua is there and beckoning.

Today I spotted a buoy in the sea and tried to retrieve it. It was an old fishing gear marker with a transmitter aerial on it and a length of wire or rope underneath. A huge gathering of Myrtle type fish and others were attending underneath, so it must have been in the water for some time to set up the food chain. I managed to grab the aerial on the way past, but the weight of the whole thing was too much and it was pulled out of my grasp. The trouble is that you have only one chance to catch something like that, the wind and waves are too powerful to row back against. We have accumulated a modest collection of debris so far, but there may well be more stuff to pick up as we approach land.

The second bottle of lime cordial has been opened. The first one was officially opened on 3 April, so the remaining two will have to be dealt with frugally if they are to last me all the way.

Whomsoever sent a text message telling me that it is their birthday on May 12, please get in touch again, I am now aiming for that date and we may well have a beer.

One click

To Antigua 888

Saturday 16 April
My breakfast of raspberry flapjack crumbled with blueberries, the last of the dates and dried apricots and full milk was being heartily enjoyed this morning when Scotty came in from engineering.
" Captain d'ye remember that dodgy supermarket we visited on our last trip to Starfleet command?"

"I remember it well Scotty, I seem to recall purchasing some waterproof loudspeakers."

"Well I just found these in my cabin"

Scotty held out a grubby box with masking tape hanging off the sides.

"Dilithium crystals captain, they arenae the proper Starfleet ones but their own brand."

"Stick em in Scotty, let's see what happens"

"Aye aye captain" Scotty beamed as he rushed away, and carelessly let a label drop as he left. On examination it read "Two for the price of one". Canny man Scotty.

Well we managed warp factor two for the day, giving us three knots when required, but squally weather has hampered us today, let's hope Scotty's crystals last longer than my speakers.

The flapjacks are so good and so easy to prepare in the mornings that I am going to half them and put a porridge mix in each half. That should make them last a little longer. After that it is scrambled eggs for brekky each day, which means more fuss. By the time the eggs run out we shall be just about there, so no breakfast for a few days only.

A ship came by yesterday without me seeing it, but I knew it was there before the Sea Me picked it up. My olfactory senses must be sharp after three months of fresh air.

The first smell was hydrocarbons; the exhaust from it's engine, then a smell which I always associate with large scale catering, but for some reason not school dinners. Despite my searching the horizon, the ship never came into view, and the Sea Me went quiet an hour later.

Thanks for the message Jeff, very reassuring.

One click

To Antigua   846

Sunday 17 April

Today has been a fairly leisurely affair by recent standards, rowing began at 0900 and proceeded with numerous breaks throughout the day, producing about thirty miles, which will be added to during the night and tomorrow morning by a drift of about 1.5 knots. A couple of squalls came through, which hampered us a little, but a generally good day for rowing.

Breakfast with the half flapjack was okay, I added plenty of dried milk powder and a spoonful of canarian honey, which I found during a locker clean. There are only two flapjacks left after tomorrows, so it will then be the eggs, (freeze dried powdered eggs).

My mileage is holding up well, so I have stopped rowing in the dark, if the miles drop off

I will start again.

It has become too hot to sleep in the cabin. If the night time temperature stays like this I shall have to make up a bunk on deck and swap places with some equipment. The snag is that the deck often gets waves break over onto it and each day I have to clear lots of dead flying fish, which have landed there during the night. Sleep can't be easy with all that going on.

The fish are too small to eat.

Nine clicks

To Antigua 806nm

Monday 18 April

Not a hint of warp drive from Scotty today, I just rowed and left him to his engines; he can be difficult when pestered. Impulse drive wasn't brilliant but I didn't dare tell him. The sea has been very changeable and difficult to row, with varying winds and waves from all directions. Maximum boat speed was two knots. Maybe tomorrow will see us back in the current.

The time difference is showing clearly here now, as I type it is 2115 hrs here and 2215 at home in Norwich. Here though, the sun is still well up and will not set for another half hour. The time changes one hour for every fifteen degrees travelled east or west. When we arrive in Antigua I will have to put my watch back four hours. That makes sense, I left the Greenwich meridian and Antigua lies at 62 degrees west.

Back on the sixth of March I mentioned to you that we had an exciting navigational moment when we entered box seven on my routeing chart and that the boxes are in reverse order counting down to Antigua. Remember? Of course you do. Well tomorrow or Wednesday we leave box three and enter box two. Excited? Good.

The routeing chart is Admiralty 5124(2) (February), should any of you wish to check my progress. Don't look for the boxes, I put them on there.

It is my intention to scrub the bottom of the boat again tomorrow, the wind is forecast to moderate during the afternoon and a swim will be in order. Keeping the hull smooth is one method of making miles.

Thank you for your messages my dear niece Sarah, your unique and refreshing view of the world keeps me uplifted.

Thanks Lorenzo, I shall be there on the first.

23 clicks

To Antigua   772

Tuesday 19 April
The wind had died away this morning after a very rough night, so I went for a swim and cleaned the hull, but there was very little to do. When I began rowing I found that there was very much to do. We were in an eddy taking us south west at 1.8 knots. It stayed like that all day, until seven tonight when a wind blew up which helped us along the way. I feel pretty sure we are clear of it now, but today has been a very hard slog.

The waves last night managed to soak me well and tonight we have some wet gear still.

Whilst typing this I fell asleep, please forgive a short bulletin this evening.

Well done John Peck for completing the marathon des sables, an incredible achievement. Ali I don't know how you got on, please let me know.

One click

To Antigua   747nm

Wednesday 20 April
These eddies are jolly difficult sometimes. We are still in it, and today has been another slog , and I have no idea when we will

exit. They play a game of cat and mouse; the rowing effort in the eddy is heavy, and when leaving the effort required drops off, giving the water a soft and light feel. The eddy has a number of areas like that to tease you with. When you have been in soft water for an hour, you think you have cleared it and just as the cigars are being passed around the water again turns to clay and the boat speed plummets. Ha Ha says eddy, gotcha still. Several areas of soft water were laid on for my amusement today, so that it will take a whole day of soft water to convince me that we are out.

Henry Dale, ocean rower of ORS 2004 regatta has kindly given me a copy of his log to read whilst I am on my way. One day at a time was my plan, but the journeys have been so remarkably similar that I have had to start reading ahead. It was beginning to look as though I was using his log for inspiration for mine, so I now check ahead to make sure that an event reported by me is not mirrored in Henry's log. Given that we are doing pretty much the same thing I suppose the stories are bound to be similar. Henry did have an experience which has so far eluded me; he had a magical encounter with a pod of killer whales. Sharks and large whales are at the top of my wannasee list, and we still have 700 miles to go.

Ian, we will have to enjoy that pint when I arrive back home, your birthday is my target day for Antigua.

Five clicks

To Antigua 715

Thursday 21 April
Three months at sea today

A vicious squall is passing over us at the moment so I take this opportunity to begin my bulletin. The squalls and eddies of the last few days (yes we are still in it) have set us back a bit, so the three quarter way mark will pass tomorrow, not today. Just as well, I'm not quite ready for the party.

About half an hour ago I was looking out to starboard at a normal kerfuffle on the surface of the sea (just a dorado catching a flying fish) when suddenly the dorado streaked like a torpedo towards the boat and slammed very hard into the side. Peering over the side and hoping to be able to lift supper out of the sea I could see nothing but the other dorado who had gathered to see what the fuss was about. He must be made of extremely stern stuff to survive a whack such as that, or perhaps he sunk.

Today the rain was so heavy that I could not see the compass to steer the boat, so rowing was suspended for a while. During the deluge I scrubbed my way around the boat letting nature take care of rinsing down.

A quick inventory of desserts this evening to see if we had enough to get into harbour; four cheesecake mixes, six vanilla and raspberry puddings and sixteen wild berry and yoghurt puddings. Easy peasy yum yum. For celebrations such as tomorrow and the seven eighths of the way mark, we also have a Christmas pudding, which I bought at a charity auction in December (£60, is that a good price?). I know it will be a good one because my mate Tim made it and he doesn't mess about. Tomorrow, my intention is to carve a big chunk out of it and pour one of the vanilla and raspberry desserts over it.

The last of the raspberry flapjacks has been consumed. (Please leave by the nearest available exit). Thank you Paul, they were simply excellent.

My short wave radio has just about had enough of short waves and is probably not going to survive much longer, when it does go I wonder if I will be relieved at not having to try tuning in to the world service.

If the present conditions do not get worse, then I may still be on schedule for arrival on 12 May, I hope to be able to firm up on the date in about three weeks time.

14 clicks

To Antigua 688

Friday 22 April
Scotty said nothing at breakfast today, but there was something about his demeanour, which led me to think he was happy about something. When I reached the rowing seat I found that the cunning old fox had fixed the warp drive. We are out of the eddy and made three knots all day, tailing off to 2.7 at finish time 8pm. Hurrah for that.

At 1300 hrs we passed the three quarter of the way mark, which is being celebrated in Womble style with a sumptuous banquet in the cockpit. My German rye bread had gone mouldy, but was ok after a trim, my penultimate container of Rioja has a certain vinegary edge to it, but is drinkable. We also have jumbo olives, a jar of mayonnaise, salami, pasta primavera and Christmas pudding, which will be smothered in vanilla and raspberry dessert.

For the last two days the wind has been blowing steadily from the south east, which is unheard of in this parish. They were not forecast but they have even had the cheek to bring their own cloud streets with them as if they were legitimate trade winds!

"What are you then?"

"We're the south east trades"

"Impossible, you don't exist"

"We do now, everything was up for grabs, so our governors did a management buy out and got the trade wind contract, so here we are"

"So what about the famous north east trades"

"Dunno mate, not our problem"

A tropic bird visited today, was trying to board, but found no space and left. So much more civilised that those commonest of Terns.

Thank you for your message David and Wendy, I'm looking forward to seeing you again, we have a lot to discuss, I think..

Ali, very well done in the London marathon, heroic stuff.

Three clicks

To Antigua 645 nm

Saturday 23 April
Not brilliant rowing today, the current was in my favour, but this south easterly pseudo trade wind remains and causes loss of speed and just spoils things.

The Dorado have gone. All of them. They were here last night all fifty of rhem, and this morning they were nowhere to be seen. Two malevolent looking barracuda are hanging around, but I can't believe they had anything to do with it, they have been around for a while. We must have drifted past something which had a well established food chain and stayed to feast on it. They will be missed. I enjoyed watching them surf the waves beside me as I did the same, and I enjoyed having them with me as escort. In the same way we do when one of the cats goes walkabout, I shall be on the foredeck shaking a bag of dried flying fish shouting "Dory Doos where are yooos?"

Myrtle has gone too.

The celebrations went well last night. The banquet, though, was enough for three people and I consumed far too much.
Our next and last milestone is seven eights of the way and we should reach that in about nine days. Yippee another banquet.
Two Manx Shearwaters have arrived and sit nearby on the water. Preliminary ID only.

A ship appeared on the horizon today and was gone again is ten minutes. No contact. The world goes about its business and knows nothing of you. Splendid isolation.

One click

To Antigua 603

Sunday 24 April
Good rowing today, the current and wind were both more
favourable and the miles came along easily. A lovely day, sunshine
and a cool breeze.

We have covered more than sixty miles since the Dorado left so
they have no chance of finding us now, however today we were
joined by three Myrtles.

Rowers who arrived in Barbados last year told me that the local
fishermen knew to fish beside the rowing boats as they arrived, and
the Dorado made the journey all the way only to be caught. It is just
as well that they have left, I'm sure the Antigua fishing community
will be doing just the same. The fish caught in the Caribbean dine
on the smaller fish which in turn have eaten weed and goodies from
coral reefs, which produce dinoflagellates. These produce a toxin
called Ciguatera, which can be poisonous to man. Fish which arrive
from the ocean are therefore less likely to cause illness.

Last night we were treated to a spectacular meteor, which lit up the
sky. You don't see that very often in Norwich.

My Christmas pudding is truly excellent and is large enough to last
me a few days. Thank you Tim, book me in for another this year
please, but we'll haggle over the price.

Erden, good to hear from you, good luck with your row, if you want
to contact me before you go, my regular number is somewhere on
the site. I will be arriving in Antigua around the 12th of May.

Two clicks

To Antigua 569

Monday 25 April
As a newspaper such as the Sun would say, today was a sizzler. 116 degrees on the rowing position, and 98 in the shade, but there ain't no shade. (These are Fahrenheit, to arrive at Celsius subtract 30 and divide the remainder by 2). Too hot to row with no wind this afternoon so I took a break and did some odd jobs, one of which was to find the charts for Antigua and begin to make plans for my approach. It looks very straightforward so long as I avoid that age old hazard of the navigator; land. Seriously, if the wind and current are normal on the day it should be easy.

Today's hallucination was the sound of the bins being emptied this morning; the diesel engine accompanied by voices and clatter. At least it wasn't the bottle recycler.

Another odd job was to stow away all my clothes, which I will no longer require on the trip; this was nearly all of them, since hardly any of them fit me now. When you are trying to imagine how skinny I look, think Ghandi.

Today I tuned in to a good solid station which did not waver on its frequency, was clear and audible and was broadcasting in English from the Caribbean with good local content. The station was the BBC world service, which surprised me a little. Thirty minutes later it was switched off and I have heard nothing of it since, and that surprises me not at all.

A Bulwers petrel came by today and showed lots of interest in us, he even sat on the sea nearby. Also, without the Dorado the boat is being visited by many more flying fish.

Thank you for your messages Thruster, Neil and Lorenzo. Alex it will be brilliant if you can make it, see you there!

Seven clicks

To Antigua   538

Tuesday 26 April

Rowing today was more difficult than usual; the wind and current were at right angles to each other, which made our top speed 2.5 knots, but the sea was very heavy going. We still made a fairly good mileage, but my limbs will be hurting tomorrow.

In about an hour we shall pass the 500 miles to go mark, which is worth a small glass of something red. These milestones seem to be much more abundant in the second half of the voyage, it is a good job I kept some goodies until now. The next one to pass will be seven eighths of the way, which will be this weekend, when the last of my treats will be consumed.

No wildlife at all today, not a thing. That's the first day that has passed without so much as a bird.

Tomorrow a rowathon is being held at Dunston Hall in aid of the Davenport Trust. Good rowing to all entrants, there will be a prize from me for the entrant whose mileage is the closest to mine tomorrow.

Ten clicks

To Antigua 500nm

Wednesday 27 April
Following on from yesterdays rowing, today we are in the mother of all eddys; at one point today I rowed for two hours and could not make more than 0.9 knots. Tonight I will try to row from time to time and see if we can escape. Today's mileage is unlikely to be enough to keep the average up. A feeling has come over me that this journey has a few surprises left in store for us yet.

One of my two white shirts, which keep the sun from scorching my back and shoulders has fallen apart. Pity, it was one of my old favourites, but the snag is that I now have to row completely starkers whilst the other shirt goes through the laundry. At least I have plenty of sun block.

A confession

Today, whilst on patrol in the galley locker, I discovered a jar of peanut butter. In order to check that it was still edible, I opened it and took a small sample with a teaspoon. One thing led to another and in a short time there was no longer a jar of peanut butter at all. I have since felt deeply guilty and gluttonous.

Dinner tonight was an undeserved pasta primavera followed by wild berries and yoghurt dessert.

Tonight I have a special mention and heartfelt thanks for a lady at Buckingham Street Day centre in Hull. This lady has been printing out my daily diary and has put it into a folder each day for my Aunty Glad. Thank you very much Freda.

Thank you for your kind words Mike Hoyland and family, also thanks to Sal and Pete and Judy and Paul.

Twenty clicks

To Antigua 471

Thursday 28 April
You will by now be familiar with the term 'we are still in it'. At four thirty this morning I began rowing to try to get some miles towards the "whereabouts unknown" edge of the eddy. After an hour or so of sheer back-break against the current I took shelter from a rain shower for a few minutes. At nine thirty I woke exactly where I had sat down. My body clock has lost synchronisation with reality and I sometimes fall asleep during the day, whilst rowing. The odd thing is that when I do so, I don't feel particularly tired.

Dorado news
Three new Dorado joined us today, as did several Myrtles. These Dorado are very quiet compared to the last lot, we'll see how they settle in. Two tropic birds and four Wilson's storm petrels today, also a large bird which I have not identified, but may be a shearwater. Thirty or so small flying fish to clear from the deck this morning. Their numbers would drop dramatically if the navigation light was switched off, but this is a shipping lane and we need to be seen, especially with rip van winkle in charge.

Neil Oxenbury has kindly offered to let me know when the election fever has gone away and it is safe to come home. Thanks Neil, much appreciated; this may be a drastic way to miss it all, but it is well worth it.

One click

To Antigua   449nm

Friday 29 April
Happy bank holiday weekend everyone

A long rowing shift today, it is past midnight and I just finished, having rowed a mere twenty miles. This eddy is a monster. We have had two small teasers to give us false hope of an end to it, but during the course of the day we didn't get the speed over 1.7 knots. Checking the ships log, I find that we have been through eddies about once per week, and they usually take three or four days to get through. That means that when we clear this one we will still have time for at least one more before landfall. What will tomorrow bring?

Whilst looking for something on deck this morning I discovered a small flying fish which had been there a while and had dried out, so I ate it. Jolly tasty it was, a bit like anchovy. I am now looking at my menus to see if we can incorporate a few of them, or I could just dry them all and eat them as snacks.

Radio Humberside called today, hello to all you listeners. I spent about five years in Hull before leaving to join the Navy, and I still have lots of family living there. The interview started me thinking about the place, and it has kept my mind occupied all day. There was once a good sized brewery in Hull called, aptly, Hull Brewery. It was in the city centre and the heady aromas which emanated therefrom were tantalising. They produced the most delicious beers and I used to really look forward to a pint when I went home on leave. One day I arrived to find that it had been taken over and shut down. What a tragedy.

For the purpose of my education I attended the Grammar School of Hull. Our school song began with the lines "Six hundred years have rolled away by Humber's swelling tide, since first our ancient walls uprose the fabric of our pride". Six hundred years was, apparently too long and the school along with the name and, I expect the pride, has gone the same way as the brewery. Nostalgia ain't what it used to be.

Wendy, I do remember the giant womble, but I can't remember where I got it from. I do however recall travelling a long journey with it. Long journey with Womble. hmmmm

One click

To Antigua 427

Sunday 1 May

Sorry about there being no diary yesterday, I rowed very late trying to clear the eddy and was completely exhausted when I finished. This morning the eddy had grabbed back five of my very hard won miles and it took until 11am to get us back to where we left off last night. This is day six in this eddy, and I'm not sure what to expect next. The last two or three days have been the hardest of the trip so far. We have been set back at least three days on my hoped for day of arrival in Antigua, and it would seem that more setbacks will occur. It would be good to arrive before my family have to leave.

Two dolphins came by this morning, what joy to see them, but they were gone in a second. Lots of small fish jumping and the ocean has come back to life. We have just passed the 400 miles to go mark, so the wildlife should be more plentiful from here on. Yesterday an albatross or something very like it came to see us, the nearest I can find in my guide is the Bullers albatross, but I shall have to spend more time on it. A fabulous bird with a wingspan of more than a metre, a black head, yellow beak, white collar, white belly and petrel colours on the upper wings.

More dried flying fish on the menu today, I wish I had started eating them earlier. One of them had rather obligingly flown into my frying pan. Now there's a considerate fish. The frying pan though, is out of action for a few days; the last of the gas cylinders was fitted this morning, but I want to conserve the gas in case I need it badly in the closing stages, so everything is cold at the moment.

The oranges seem a long time ago.

I wonder what I will remember and what I will forget of this odyssey. Hopefully bits like the last three days will be cast into the recycle bin and the rest stored in the hard drive and backed up somewhere.

Thank you all for your messages, Chris and Maureen, Julie, Andrew, Barbara, George, Sally and Pete, Judy and Paul. keep them coming please.

Sally I want to keep the diary going until I return to Norwich to record my thoughts and events on my return. After that I shall probably let it go, but have a news page for things which are worth mentioning in the months to come.

No cooking today, so no clicks.

To Antigua 399

Monday 2 May
The wretched eddy spat us out like a cherry stone at about three this morning and we have been a escape velocity since then. It seems crazy to stop rowing until we are a thousand miles from the thing in case we are dragged back in. My rowing routine has gone by the wayside until we are well clear and, probably ready to get into the next one which hopefully won't be as strong. The thing was over a hundred miles across and held us for six days, turning the boat around and sending us backwards, sideways and any which way. It should be marked with a large sign.

Last night I rowed until 1am, had a doze, then from 3 until 6am, breakfast and doze until 9, when the big row for the day began. A one hour break at five pm, then rowing through until midnight. Diary, shower, snooze and so on.

After all my fine words about conserving gas, I had to use some this morning for my eggs; they need to be cooked, everything else is ok cold.

Along with the eddy and a westerly wind last night we also had an electrical storm nearby, just to add value for the evening. That gave me a bit of an anxious time, how close do you let these things get before you stop rowing and shelter? The text of the section on carbon fibre oars would probably go " Carbon fibre, if struck, will atomise and any person sitting nearby will be instantly vapourised". My decision was to stay and row, and eventually the storm moved away.

Arrival is beginning to excite me a little; I have a number of jobs to do and people to see, but I look forward to so many things. Just a few:
Fresh fruit
A big bath
Learning to walk again (it's been nearly four months)
A stationary bed
Food, that stays on its plate
A proper lavatory
Muesli
Sitting still
Curry
Iced orange juice
Rum punch

The three Dory doos have gone, they were very different to the last lot, no style at all.

No clicks

To Antigua   353

Tuesday 3 May
Good rowing today, not bad conditions, but yesterday was a corker, we managed about 55 miles, which seems unreal after all that messing about in the eddy. Our last milestone fell this morning at 1100. We are now more than seven-eighths of the way to Antigua, and so in true Womble fashion tonight we are to have a gianagerous feast with all of the treats kept back from the voyage. No titbit picnic this, we are going to give it the full flying circus. We even have a few liquorice allsorts left.

Today must be something like day 103, and I have done a couple of odd jobs which for some unfathomable reason have not been done until now. One of them was to screw down the footplate which for well over a million rowing strokes has made a clunk as I row. Another was to make a very simple backrest for the rowing position which means I can now take a breather without getting up, and I can lay back at night and stargaze. At this late stage I also fitted the last pair of oar handle grips, which are exceedingly comfortable. Thank you David Cosford.

One Wilsons petrel today and one small gold fish. Not a big day for nature appreciation.

Tonight I would like to thank Elizabeth Beresford, creator of the Wombles, for allowing me to name the boat Womble and for her kind words of support. These are on display in the pub. I would also like to thank Nat Spring and Justin Coleman for giving me the 'Wombling across the ocean' inspiration. Nat and Justin were crew members on boats in the ORS regatta last year.

One click

To Antigua 312

Wednesday 4 May
Scotty has been insufferable these last two days, hanging around in the control room with a stupid smirk on his face. "Everything alright Captain?" he says from time to time.

"Yes" is the only reply he gets, he is smug about the warp drive. We have had warp speed for the last couple of days, which has come in very handy. The track is still a bit too far south, but that should be fixed in the next few days. Funny how we never saw Scotty when the Klingons were trying to drag us into that space – time anomaly. He must have been reading too much Para Handy and thinks he is a real engineer like McPhail.

A container ship was on our bearing this morning, thankfully he answered the VHF and altered course without mowing us down. Afterwards I was thinking that the Womble will be on its way back to the UK in a couple of weeks time on a ship just like that.

Remember the boxes on the chart? We are now half way through box one; the last box. There then remains about a hundred miles to Antigua, and rum punch.

Earlier I discovered two tins of chilli. They opened quite easily and just filled my big bowl nicely. Then I ate them, with a huge dollop of mayonnaise. Wow.

Ever the optimist, I brought out the music system to see if the passage of time had healed the burnt out electronics, but the answer was a sorry silence. This next week should be exciting enough as we approach the island, but to have the music again would be really welcome. The radio is just about moribund; only the sleep button will turn it on, and its batteries must be removed to turn it off. It cannot stay on station for any time and needs more nursing than a baby.

The symptoms of Ciguatera (24 April) have been enquired after by someone who presumably thinks he or she might be exposed to it. I looked them up in the cruising guide and they sound very much like the symptoms of nerve gas poisoning or drinking too much tequila; nausea, vomiting, abdominal pain, and diarrhoea and can lead to paralysis and death. The only cure is to make the sufferer vomit until their stomach is empty. One hopes that there is someone around to make you puke before the death bit settles in.

No clicks

To Antigua 265

Thursday 5 May
Congratuations Bob and Dani on the birth of your daughter.

After early poor conditions we had a huge improvement this afternoon and found both wind and current. The forecast for the weekend is good and my confidence is increasing that we will make Antigua next Thursday. It does not seem real yet that the journey is coming to an end. I am getting excited, but there are over two hundred miles yet to row. Very real miles, which can be easy or hard. The general buzz of anticipation will no doubt kick in when the miles are less than a hundred.

My sleep has been minimal for a few days, due mostly to the sea state. The wind is forecast to moderate soon so I should be able to catch up on my zeds before we arrive. It would be a pity to arrive and want to do nothing but sleep.

We have a guest onboard; it is a Brown Noddy, a very pretty little seabird with a pale grey forehead, brown plumage and black or very dark brown tail. It arrived this evening and will probably be gone tomorrow.

We are presently listening to election night coverage on radio Pluto, and so far we have two constituencies declared. Could be a long night.

Dinner tonight is cold chicken teryaki, but I am treating myself to a double wild berry and yoghurt dessert.

No clicks, To Antigua 228.

Friday 6 May
Today we were caught in a current, which wanted to take us south and steal yesterdays hard earned northings. Rowing steadfastly through the day, I had to stop for body fuel at 2000. Fifteen minutes later the current had altered to the west and is now helping us towards Antigua.

A Sooty Shearwater arrived on the scene today, last nights Noddy has gone. Sooty is a fine powerful bird. Noddy had a big wingspan and looked impressive in the sky, yet folded up as small as a pigeon when he landed.

The last lime cordial came out today as we have now less than 200 miles to go. Also brought out was a large bottle of mandarin juice, which is unlikely to survive tomorrow. Very few treats left now, and the food list has shrunk to a level which would have the rats jump ship if we had any.

A large motor vessel the Coral Sea came past today, we spoke on the VHF, but their radar did not pick up our sea me, nor did we detect it. Worrying.

Last night was very rough and I slept hardly at all again. The howling banshees outside can make it difficult even for the very tired to sleep through. Shutting the hatch would help, but I seem to consume all of the oxygen in the cabin in a very short time.

Thank you for your kind messages Mike and the crew at the Coach and Horses, Thorpe Road, a fine establishment, Ian Shreeve, Ali Boreham, Mike and Claire Farnworth (I'll be in touch soon) .

No clicks

To Antigua 189nm

Saturday 7 May
Difficult rowing again today, the winds and seas were high and I had trouble keeping a course. The forecast is more of the same, so it looks as if the last few days of the trip are going to be as tough as any.

Sleep was zero again last night; the sea me started alarming at midnight and went on for an hour before the ship came into view. It passed harmlessly a mile away with no contact. I had to settle for a nap at about six this morning, having been thrown savagely around the cabin for the remainder of the night.

My last packet of rye bread was opened this afternoon, and was fresh as new. Spread with almogrote, mayonnaise and a chunk of corned beef it was scrum yum.

Remember the boxes on the chart? Of course you do, well tomorrow night we leave the last box (number one) and we will just have the last hundred miles or so to row into the harbour. Just like that. Let's hope so, I have more worries about the last two days than the rest of the trip.

Last week at the four hundred miles to go mark, I called my wife to say that we were effectively leaving Glasgow for Norwich, and that I would tell her daily where we had reached. Today we have just passed Boroughbridge on the A1. We came down the M8, M74, A74 to Carlisle, then to Penrith and onto the A66 over Bowes moor. We will carry on down to Sleaford where we will leave the A1 and head East. This is absolute tosh and nonsense of course, rowing boats are not allowed to use the queen's highway and I do not require any text messages suggesting alternative routes, thank you. I'll let you all know when we reach Swaffham.

No clicks

To Antigua 150nm

Monday 9 May
Again, apologies for no diary yesterday, I have been rowing constantly to try to extricate us from the latest and biggest eddy yet. This one has taken us around the compass, thirty and more miles North of Antigua and is presently whisking us North East at over one knot. To date my strategy for dealing with these has been to row west. This one is so strong that I can get only 0.4 knots West with full effort. I have decided to stop rowing against it and conserve energy for when it turns in my favour or we somehow get out of it

Yesterday I rowed firstly for fifteen hours, then through the night on and off which made eighteen hours, then today I have rowed ten hours so far. It is tantalising too think that Antigua, family and friends are only 118 miles away, but I am being taken further away.

Today I saw a shark fin behind the boat and when I looked, it was a twelve foot bull shark with a big bluff nose. A quick photo and back to the oars. He found the boat fascinating and stayed for half an hour, just moseying around. Tick the box on that one, just a large whale now, and my wannasee list is complete.

Things I am not looking forward to:

Tobacco smoke
Other air pollution
Fast cars
Lists
Television

That's about all, so life doesn't frighten me that much.

Tonight we have our first radio station on medium wave; good local music and great stuff.

No clicks

To Antigua 119

Tuesday 10 May
The Klingons may well have won this time; we travelled forty four miles North and fifteen miles East since they grabbed us and still we head east at 1.5 knots. I have spent many hours trying to arrest the

movement, but to no avail. Sadly this could be the end of the attempt. The food will last me a week at a push, but each day we move east adds a days rowing into the equation for landfall. By my calculations Antigua is now five days rowing away. If no change happens in the next 24 hours I shall have to arrange a re-supply or a tow in.

The medium wave radio station is now, of course out of range again.

No clicks

To Antigua 135, and rising.

Thursday 12 May
Today was to have been arrival day, but never mind. Yesterday was spent trying to arrange a tow, whilst trying to arrange things so that we did not need a tow. My wife was in Antigua carrying out the first part, whilst I busied myself with the second. By last night, Neet had not only arranged a tow by the Royal Navy, she had found two of my old Navy muckers to boot. For my part, I formulated a plan, made some rules, made preparations and executed said plan.

My position was well to the North, but because I had been rowing against the drift for most of the time, we did not go too far East. The plan was to row us out of the eddy no matter how long it took or how slow the rate of escape. No sleeping or breaks, and all eating and drinking to be done on the move. Plenty of eats and drinks were laid on and my task began. The intended route was south west, I turned the boat and began. The water felt like granite and we moved South West at 0.1 to 0.2 knots for the first five hours. This crept up as the day and night wore on, until at 1130 last night when we were making 1 knot. When I stopped rowing, I looked at the speed display to find that we were no longer being taken backwards. I was exhausted and so tried to take a nap, but I slept very little. At 0230 Radio Norfolk called to do an interview after which I began rowing again. Solid hours through until 1700 this evening when the boat speed had reached 1.5 knots. Neet has called off the Navy, (Thank you Commander Kerr) and I think we can say that tomorrow we should be clear and on our way. All of this is just to show you how industrious I have been, and why I deserved to eat a whole jar of peanut butter this evening. My appetite has never been so keen.

Jeff, my cousin and hero sent me a text message this morning detailing the location of all the eddies in the area, including the one we were in. Because they have no visual features, it is impossible to know the layout and shape of eddies, but with Jeff's info we were able to plan the great escape. Thanks Jeff, the milky bars are on me when we meet next, which will, I hope be soon.

The night before last I was rowing late when I heard dolphins. They were all around the boat and stayed for fifteen minutes before leaving. The phosphorescence when they jump and turn is magical. Another great event at the ringside, and it wasn't even on my list.

The text messages I received today after the radio interviews were very heartwarming, thank you all.

One click

To Antigua, 117 nm, and falling.

Friday 13 May
A particularly inauspicious day to spend at sea in a rowing boat. As you all know, we Sagittarians don't believe in all this stuff, but for

an Albatross to fly over your head as soon as you get out of your cabin on Friday the thirteenth, well what luck can you expect? Try this; at first rowing we were back into the big eddy but a different zone. The whole day has been spent trying to row out of it, and trying to estimate where it ends.

You must be getting fed up of this; I know I am. Still, if we didn't have bad luck, we would have no luck at all! That would not do. My intention is to grab a quick hour's sleep now, and get cracking again to try to have us released before dawn. We will then have a full days work ahead.

Thank you all for your calls and messages.

One click

To Antigua 100

Saturday 14 May
We finally exited the big Ed this morning, and with help from cousin Jeff I have sketched the hideous creature on my chart. It is actually the same one which we first ran into on the 6th of May. On that day it was trying to take us South, but with lots of effort I managed to keep us on track. When we were carried away on the 7th May the eddy was on its way North. Had I stayed in it for a few more days, I would have gone around in a huge ovoid and ended up where I began. The left side of it, which we spent so much time getting across was over thirty miles wide. With luck we should not encounter too much more in the way of current. Tonight I ran out of steam completely whilst rowing, I was hallucinating so much that I could not row properly. I was convinced that an ice cream kiosk was behind my right shoulder and kept trying to avoid it.

Antigua sounds very pretty and a most agreeable place to land. It is now only 85 miles away and I think I can just about smell rum.

The short wave radio received its biggest and probably its last wave today, it has done rather well, all things considered. It was designed for domestic use only, and I remember the man in the shop where I bought it years ago telling me that it should not be played for more than four hours a day. No, I couldn't work it out either.

There have been so many birds here in the last few days that I haven't had time to identify, they are so beautiful and the larger ones are truly spectacular, and then we have the common Tern.

No clicks

To Antigua 85nm and falling

Sunday 15 May
Out of the fat......

A fresh current caught us as we headed South west towards the seventeen degree line and took us North, then North East and we spent the whole day trying to crab out of it, which was achieved at 2300 this evening. Just another day

Today as a sort of clear up, I gathered all the food remaining onboard and piled it up in the cabin. Not a big pile. The best way to ration it is, I think, to allocate so much for each ten miles. Good that's one pack of freeze dried food per ten. Very fair.

The Davenport trust

The Davenport trust is a fledgling charity which I have adopted and for which I intend to continue raising funds in forthcoming years. The charity was founded by James Clarke and is based at Old Westwick Hall. The funds raised in the course of my row will enable the building of the headquarters and give the charity help to start meeting its aims, which are to raise the awareness of the symptoms of depression in young people and to eventually help young people who suffer from the illness.

The charity takes its name from Shaun Davenport who took his own life in tragic circumstances in 2003. Shaun was unaware of his illness and the symptoms were not obvious; disguised among normal adolescent behaviour

If you wish to donate to the trust, the details are elsewhere on this site, however the option to donate online is not yet available.

No clicks

To Antigua 62nm and falling

Monday 16 May
This morning at 0300 as we rowed away from yesterdays entertainment we found today's. A current, not on cousin Jeff's latest chart, sprung up and began taking us North. This as I was lining up for final approach into Antigua. As I type, we await the abatement of a strong southerly wind (not forecast) to see if any headway can then be made for the harbour. Plan B will be to go to Barbuda instead, but I do not like plan B; it is complicated and I have no contacts there. Plan C is a tow, but that will only be done when all other options are exhausted.

The dangerous parts of any sea voyage are the start and the finish. My navigation must be precise, but I must also have a number of other things correctly attended to before I contemplate landfall. The hatches must all be tightly shut, the water ballast must all be in place and secured. My safety equipment must be ready to wear, and my VHF radios must be fully charged and ready to use. My charts and pilot book should be at hand, also my passage plan. The Antigua courtesy flag should be raised, also flag Q, a yellow flag which alerts customs. Fenders for the sides should be ready, also docking lines and springs. The towing rope should be out and ready to use. The decks must be cleared so that I can move around easily. Since I will be rowing continuously, a supply of drinks must be ready beside me with some handy snacks if I have anything left by then. Just for good measure, as I enter harbour I will have a movie camera filming and my still camera ready. Lastly but certainly not least, I must have all my ships papers ready for customs to inspect on arrival.

I'm getting excited now.

<u>Stop press</u> (I've always wanted to do that)

At 1300 the current turned to the North East and gained speed, this wiped out my last chance of rowing to any of the islands in the chain and at 1330 I called my wife and asked her to arrange a tow. I would like to point out that this is not a rescue; it is a commercial tow paid for by myself and no calls have been made on any emergency services.

It is such a shame that it should work out this way; the harbour was a mere 49 43nm away when we were at our closest point. However I am perfectly happy with what I have done; I have crossed the Atlantic in my rowing boat and if anyone thinks I haven't, they should get out more. I did quite a bit of it twice and some of it three times for heaven's sake.

As I sit here waiting for my tow, a school of dolphins, twenty or so, with one youngster and an appetite for Dorado, has visited me. The Dolphins are rather good at catching them, they approach from the blind side of the boat at great speed and then turn upwards to take them as they hide on the other side.

The short wave radio was dead, so I recycled the loudspeaker and my MP3 player is entertaining me again. I expect to have to wait some time for my tow, so the music is really welcome.

The tow will be here at 0200, so I have had a special supper saved for the last night of the trip. Haggis, potatoes, and the last miniature of Malt whisky.

Seventeen clicks

To Antigua 49 43nm

Tuesday 17 May
Happy birthday to my dear sister Wendy. We said it would be today, did we not?

At 0500 the tow boat arrived, a magnificent former RNLI lifeboat circa 1954. The Sea Terror belongs to Chris Harris and his daughter Scarlett who live onboard. My youngest brother Andrew helped me to board, and within minutes we were on our way through the mire and clag and heading for ANTIGUA. This though, came as I realised that for a day or so I had been able to see the island at night. The strange glow in the sky at one spot was the island lights, and we were heading towards the glow. Another glow to the left was Guadeloupe.

The Womble towed without any trouble and whilst we travelled I took my first nap for a long time on the upper deck of the Sea Terror. The movement of the boat was a stark contrast to the violent movement of a rowing boat and I was gently rocked to sleep in a very short time. After an hour I woke and began trying to walk around the deck. It was not easy and I bumped into things and reeled around as if drunk; my balance mechanism was in disrepair. As we approached the island I chatted to Chris about the eddies and the currents around the area, he pointed to the GPS as we went along saying that we had just lost or gained a knot here and there. We were transiting more eddies. By now I would have been wombling my way to Greenland.

When we reached the island a large number of boats were gathering for a regatta, I transferred back to the Womble and made my preparations to row into harbour. As I rowed, the boats gathered around us and people began clapping. This was no regatta, we were to be escorted into harbour!

After an emotional mid water family reunion we continued in to Nelson's Dockyard and tied alongside at 1530. A huge crowd was gathered on the quayside and I was met by the Deputy High Comissioner Mr Paul Lawrence, who escorted me through the customs and immigration formalities. My balance had not yet recovered though, and I had to be supported by my daughters. The media interviews and the obligatory cold beer photo shots over, we retired to a shady terrace at the waterside of the Admiral's Inn for rum punches and family chat. Exquisite feelings all round. Womble was then moved for me to the Inn quay, where she sits enjoying the sunshine and admiring gaze of tourists and residents.

In the evening I was invited to address a formal reception and to meet the Minister for tourism. During the reception a call was received from the Ocean Rowing Society in London, who informed me that they had recognised my row as complete, albeit assisted. Great news.

After a series of very flattering speeches and offers of great generosity, we returned to the hotel for dinner. In the circumstances and with great care, I selected from the menu the most appropriate dish for the evening; Dorado.

No clicks

To Antigua 0nm

Wednesday 18 May
A good night's sleep in a substantial four poster bed and a hearty breakfast is my recommended cure for the ailments incurred whilst ocean rowing. This morning I can walk unaided, albeit in a wobbly line, my fatigue is much diminished and my appetite sated. The day is a full diary of media and social appointments, the highlight being at the tot club at Galleons Beach tonight. Mmmm rum. More tomorrow.

Roll the credits.

At risk of sounding like someone at the Oscars awards, I would like to thank most sincerely everyone who has contributed to this endeavour in any way. From the big corporate sponsors to the people who put their loose change into the jar on the bar, you all had a part to play in this.

My wife Anita not only gave me domestic planning permission for the trip, she ran the pub and its kitchen, looked after our children and typed out these bulletins daily. In addition she was my sounding board and counsellor on the phone each evening. I think she deserves a special mention don't you? How many wives would allow their husbands to spend their silver wedding anniversary on an expedition?

Thursday 19th May 2005

Today has been spent tidying the boat, and getting equipment ready for shipping. My Mum and daughters return to the UK tonight, whilst Neet stays here to help me recover and prepare to return. The Antigua Yacht club have invited us to a reception this evening in aid of the Davenport Trust, for which we are very grateful.

The Antigua government is interested in having the Womble for a new museum opening soon in Nelson's Dockyard . We are trying to work out how we can do this and will post our decision soon.

Last night I rowed us over to the Tot club event, upon which my body howled with shock and anguish. Sophie expertly rowed us on the return trip

Friday 20th May 2005

The last of our family and friends leave for the UK today, Neet and myself are moving from the splendid quarters of the Admiral's Inn, where we have been lavished with hospitality, to Galleon's Beach resort.

The Admiral's Inn is a shady gem in the Georgian dockyard and we were treated like royalty by Ethelenne and all of the staff there. It was the perfect place to wind down yet at the same time be available for the media and well-wishers.

We are to be given a beach villa at the Galleon's Beach resort for the remainder of our stay, courtesy of the management, and for which we are very grateful.

The next few days will be spent taking things easy and trying to put some meat back onto my woefully skinny frame; I weighed in at 155 pounds, or eleven stones, or seventy kilos. I don't have any idea what it might be in London buses, Nelson's columns or Olympic swimming pools, but you get the drift.

The boat sits happily at the Admiral's where she will remain for the next few days and we plan to fly back to the UK ourselves next Wednesday, to arrive in Norwich on Thursday afternoon.

Added mass: 0.5 kilos, and rising.

Saturday 21st May 2005

We made our final decision on the fate of the Womble today; she is to remain in Antigua to be exhibited in the Nelson's Dockyard museum, and will be available to use again if an Antiguan or Barbudan individual or pairs team wish to enter any of the trans-Atlantic rowing races.

After making our decision, we began removing my personal gear and the remaining electronics and rowing equipment from the boat. The spread of gear which appeared on the pontoon was incredible; it is a source of amazement to me that I managed to fit all of the stuff into the boat in the first instance.

It will feel odd to leave the island without the boat, it has been a constant companion for about a year now and the stripping out phase seems harsh. No matter, all in a good cause.

Sunday 22nd May 2005
Sorry, the briefest of entries today, we have moved to the Galleon Beach resort into our villa. Mr Mark Boswell has provided us with a wonderful beachside villa and we are very busy swimming and drinking punch. Must dash.

Monday 23rd May 2005
The temperature in Antigua has soared and the whole population, visitors, natives and all, are suffering badly. Anywhere with air conditioning is curiously busy and drinks are the business to be buying into. We were lent a handsome 38 foot yacht yesterday and today we took her for a sail to get some fresh air and perhaps see an eddy to pick a fight with. No eddy was brave enough and the wind died away, but it was a most enjoyable few hours and we followed it with a magnificent curry in a local restaurant. Tomorrow will be spent packing rowing equipment into a shipping crate and getting ready to return to Norwich. We decided to burn off the remaining gas from the stove for safety reasons, and Neet did the honours with the lighter.

One click. Plus two kilos and rising...

Tuesday 24th May 2005
The crate was finished today and we began squeezing the equipment into it. A visit to St John's earlier provided some amusement; we were there to be interviewed by a local journalist in

his office at the studios of Observer radio. The interview went well, but on the way out we were accosted and marched into another studio and spent over an hour on the station live for a phone-in. The studio was air conditioned and the time went very quickly.

Back in English Harbour at six we attended a meeting of the Tot Club, a dedicated group of Royal Naval historians who re-enact the rum issue daily.

My appetite for food has caused me some concern, I seem to be uncharacteristically gluttonous and I now eat sweet things in a way I never have before. However my weight is returning and a few of the small defects incurred in the last two weeks are being cured.

Wednesday 25th May 2005

Our last day on the pretty island of Antigua, and a frantic last minute pack of crate and cases before the formal handover ceremony of the Womble at the Admiral's Inn. Speeches made and photo ops done we handed over our hire car and headed for the airport. Too late to buy a seat with leg room, we opted for the next grade of seat and were told to come back later for our boarding cards. At the appointed time we dutifully arrived and were told to return in an hour. Alarm bells began ringing in my head and an hour later we discovered that our plane was held up in an eddy in St Lucia. We were expecting a number of people back at the Alex on our arrival, some of whom had travelled long distances and it was with some disappointment that we went to a hotel for the night.

Statement and press release
By James (Tiny) Little, ocean rower.

On the 17th of May at three thirty in the afternoon, my three thousand mile journey across the Atlantic Ocean came to an end. Arriving in Antigua was both a relief and a thrill. In 1975 I visited Antigua and experienced a deep affinity for the island and its people.

The welcome I received last week was simply outstanding and was certainly not what I expected. The fleet of boats which I thought was a regatta, but were in fact my escort, was just the first part of an arrival to remember. My heartfelt thanks go to everyone who came to meet me, especially The Hon Harold Lovell, Minister of Tourism, who took time from a very busy schedule to welcome me and address the reception in the evening. Yachting liaison officer Mr Andy McDonald played a key part in the ceremonies and I thank him also.

The hospitality and support received by my family and the generous way we have been treated display the human spirit of the island people and for all this we thank you so much. Particular thanks go to the Yacht club of Antigua, the Tot club, Mr. Guy Rowsell, Mr. Chris Harris of the MV Sea Terror, Mrs. Ethelyn Phillips of the Admiral's Inn, Mr. Mark Boswell of Galleon Beach Resort, Mr. George Clarke of Antigua Yacht Services, Mr. Tino Troje-Tuck of Woodstock Boat Builders, Commander Jack Kerr Royal Navy, and Mr. Paul Lawrence, Deputy High Commissioner.

My wife and I have decided that we would like to donate my boat, the Womble, to the Island of Antigua, in the hope that it will be used as an exhibit in one of the museums, until the museum of ocean rowing is established. It is my hope that a team or individual from Antigua might enter one of the rowing races in the future, and that the Womble be made available to them for that purpose. In that event I will make myself available to offer every assistance.

In conclusion I would like to say that future ocean rowers are in for a wonderful landfall in this tropical paradise and I hope to spend many more happy times here with my family.

James (Tiny) Little

Thursday 26th May 2005
An air conditioned sleep was very welcome, but information on our flight has been scant and difficult to find. The latest is that we will be collected tonight but we have no flight time and therefore no ETA. Harrumph.

Friday 27th May 2005
Our flight finally left last night at 9.30, after a scary moment when a large crowd had gathered around the BA desk. We thought the flight was again being delayed, but it was someone else's turn. At 1030 this morning we disembarked at Gatwick and began the final stage of the journey home. Our car was waiting and we queued to leave the airport. We then queued to join the M25. The M25 had a selection of queues for our amusement as did the M11, A11 and B1180. My first experience of driving in five months proved to be an unsettling one and I was very happy to turn the corner into our road. As we approached the pub a television camera came into view, along with a jolly collection of our regular customers, suppliers and journalists. The pub looked great, having been

decorated with banners and flags. After a splendid welcome and numerous photos and interviews we settled to have a drink with each other and wind down.

Added mass, one kilo.

Saturday 28th May 2005
Straight into work mode today, Neet working the kitchen and yours truly sorting cellars. My muscles and general strength seem to have suffered. The beer barrels seem to weigh three times as much as before and I struggled to manage them. There is more to this ocean rowing business than I imagined; a much longer period of recovery than I thought may be necessary. A four mile walk to the Coach and Horses and back seemed to be easy enough, and my legs coped well, but I still cannot run without losing my balance.

Sunday 29th May 2005
Sleep patterns are returning to normal, but I have been having regular dreams about rowing since I arrived in Antigua: I am constantly trying to get down to 17 degrees north, which is very close, but unattainable. After such long nights rowing I wake up very tired. This evening we had a most agreeable chat with ocean rower Andrew Vinsen and his friend Clare, who will compete in the Woodvale / ORS race later in the year. After all the help and advice given to me by Andrew before and during my row, we had a lot to talk about.

Monday 30th May 2005
In 1997 a friend and I bought a general purpose auxiliary ship from the Royal Navy. We have operated it since then as an environmental

survey and dive support vessel, principally working on prospective windfarm sites in the North Sea. Since I left in January she has been laid up in Lowestoft and today I went down to see her and turn over the engines. It seems so different to board a vessel which does not lurch to one side at the first tentative step onto the deck. One day I shall do battle with the eddies in our valiant ship, just for the fun of it. The ship is in a shabby state and needs a few weeks of TLC before she works again. My time looks as if it is taken up for a while, but it will help me to get back into shape physically and the sea air will do me good.

Tuedsay 31st May 2005

Another day in Lowestoft, chipping, painting and general tidying. On my way to buy some light bulbs I made the mistake of trying to run across a road. My legs felt just as they do when, in a dream, I try to run away from something unpleasant but I am held back by an invisible force field. The driver of the car which narrowly missed me must have wondered what was going on.

Anyone who recognises me now makes a rowing gesture with their arms. This is recognisable by me, but onlookers must surely be perplexed.

Best wishes and smooth rowing to our local man Oliver Hicks. He has departed from New York for Falmouth and is making excellent miles. Good luck Oliver.

Wednesday 1st June 2005

The Norfolk and Norwich Licensed Victuallers Association held their annual trade lunch today, and Neet and I were invited as guests of honour. What an honour it was. The association have

adopted the Davenport Trust as their annual charity and a
substantial sum was raised during the course of the afternoon.

Thursday 2nd June 2005
This morning I took the plunge and walked into Paul's news on
Rosary Road Norwich to buy my first raspberry flapjack since my
return home. It felt quite odd as I saw the cellophane wrapped
goodies on his shelf; the last one I saw became a milestone in my
journey. My recent appetite took over and I bought two; one for
later. Ten minutes later I had consumed both, but the wonderful
flavour had taken me beyond reason and I found myself
remembering the list of other goodies I had combined with them to
form the grand breakfasts enjoyed in the second half of the trip.
Breakfast was the most important meal and required plenty of slow
release carbohydrates to feed me during the mile-munching
daytime rowing periods.

Shifting beer barrels has been part of my job for nearly twenty
years now, so it would be sensible to assume that I would be able to
get straight back into action on my return without any problems.
An eighteen gallon barrel weighs around two hundred pounds in
total and now outweighs me by far, so I am having some difficulty
doing my job. Time to get back to the gym and work on the muscles
which are not required for ocean rowing; they are well relaxed and
need stretching and developing again.

Friday 3rd June 2005
More ship based maintenance today, until the afternoon, when I
met up with Andrew Vinsen, and we took the train to London for
my first visit to the headquarters of the Ocean Rowing Society. The
occasion was a seminar for prospective ocean rowers. Nigel Gower

was the guest speaker, but as the evening progressed, Graham Walters, Andrew and myself joined the discussions and a useful amount of information was exchanged.

Saturday 4th June 2005

Henry Dale, ocean rower came to Norwich today, and we began our plans for next year, when we will row a sizeable portion of the inland waterways of Britain in a specially designed boat. Henry was a rower in last year's ORS regatta and became a solo rower when his partner Justin Coleman became ill. We have no idea how we will cope in a boat with another rower, and it will be another adventure for both of us. Our wives are planning to join us for the expedition which should be around three weeks in duration. Watch this space…

For two nights now, my rowing dreams have stopped and I am sleeping much more soundly. Hurrah for that. Just a few more minor snags to fix and I should be as good as new.

Sunday 5th June 2005

A lazy day with one of those breakfasts I could only wish for when they were out of reach. My body needs rest, exercise, food, healing time and flexibility training all at once. If I neglect any of them I am quickly reminded.

Monday 6th June 2005

Back to work, beginning with pub stuff in the morning followed by the drive to Lowestoft. The boat needs a full paint job and we are currently grinding and preparing the steelwork for the first primer coat. The work is dirty and noisy but the physical effort in climbing ladders, scraping decks, hammering chisels and generally exercising muscles which have not been used for a long time is showing results; I feel more flexible and agile. My appetite continues unabated, with bulimia style binges. My fear is that it will continue until I reach my old weight, which will simply not do.

Tuedsay 7th June 2005
Lowestoft; chipping, grinding, wire brushing, cutting, welding, chiselling, sweeping, shovelling and the first fish and chips meal of 2005.

Wednesday 8th June 2005
A phone call today informed me that we may have a job to do with the boat. This prompted a flurry of tidying and testing gear to be sure everything works. The prospect of going to sea again is rather attractive. It will be a joy to have the grunt of a large marine engine at my fingertips, dealing with the waves and tides without effort.

Thursday 9th June 2005
The job is confirmed, we sail tonight at midnight to a gas installation in the North Sea. Must dash, lots to do.

Friday 10th June 2005
Textbook stuff, the job was completed by 0900 and we headed back for Lowestoft, arriving at 1400. Everything worked and we were on our way to Norwich by 1500, having offloaded all equipment. The roll of the ship feels very gentle compared with the vicious righting lever of an ocean rowing boat.

Saturday 11th June 2005
Today I have reached the tender age of 49 and a half. Half birthdays count, don't they?

Neet and I set out early to drive to Portland in Dorset, where we attended a launching party for the sister ship to our big boat. Owned by Jim and Dee Woodward from Boston USA, the Fintry was built on the same slip, at the same time as our Dornoch. (Just a coincidence, but Jim's real name is James Little-Woodward!). We were entertained with true American hospitality and had a sail around Weymouth Bay before heading into town for a most agreeable curry. Jim and Dee have a website at mvfintry.com and we have a small information site at mvdornoch.com.

Sunday 12th June 2005
We returned to Norwich today, and spent a social afternoon at the pub.

This will be my last daily entry for a while; I shall endeavour to update on a weekly basis from now until we have some more regular exciting stuff to relate, but please do visit regularly; there are events and things afoot which may be of great interest to some of you and I don't want you to miss them.

The diary was discontinued at this point, I shifted into work mode and began other projects which have no relevance here. For some months I spoke to various groups of people who had raised funds for the Davenport Trust, and then days without a thought of rowing began to come and go.

I have fond memories of the row, the pain was all worth the pleasure of spending so much time with the sea, its natural inhabitants and the sometimes rather silly things that occupied my mind.

The most regular question asked by my supporters and others was "Why". No answer comes to mind which does not sound faintly ridiculous. It is a wonderfully pointless thing to do, but it leaves a very satisfying feeling of having achieved something which very few people have even considered.

See what I mean? Faintly ridiculous.

Tiny.

"When you are out there you will wish you had never started, but when you return you will be happy that you did it for the rest of your life".

Kenneth Crutchlow, Ocean Rowing Society International.
www.oceanrowing.com